Why the Testimonies Were Given to the Seventh-day Adventist Church

When the *Testimonies for the Church* were first published, the people and events written about were often fresh in the minds of Adventist readers. But several decades have passed by since then. The purpose of this book is to review the circumstances that first called for the counsel. But more than this—in the recalling, we can see their application for today.

After briefly relating the experiences of the Israelites as they left slavery in Egypt, the Apostle Paul says: "Now all these things happened to them as examples, and they were written for our admonition, on whom the ends of the ages have come" (1 Corinthians 10:11, NKJV).

Ellen White spoke in a similar way about her testimonies: "Since the warning and instruction given in testimony for individual cases applied with equal force to many others who had not been specially pointed out in this manner, it seemed to be my duty to publish the personal testimonies for the benefit of the church" —*Testimonies for the Church*, 5:658, 659 (hereafter identified as *Testimonies*).

The preacher chooses his sermon topic, the teacher prepares a lesson plan, the evangelist explains Bible prophecies, but not so the prophet. The Lord calls the prophet, then tells the prophet what to say, and, finally, when to say it.

Ellen White did not easily accept the Lord's call. She tells us: "When this work was first given me, I begged the Lord to lay the burden on someone else. The work was so large and broad and deep that I feared I could not do it"—*Selected Messages*, 1:32.

It didn't get easier. Writing thirty years later, she confided: "I have felt for years that if I could have my choice and please God as well, I would rather die than have a vision, for every vision places me under great responsibility to bear testimonies of reproof and of warning, which has ever been against my feelings, causing me affliction of soul that is inexpressible. Never have I coveted my position, and yet I dare not resist the Spirit of God and seek an easier position"—ibid ., 3:36, 37.

At the conclusion of her first book, Ellen White summed up her understanding of the work that God had given her: "I recommend to you, dear reader, the Word of God as the rule of your faith and practice. By that Word we are to be judged. God has, in that Word, promised to give visions in the '*last days*'; not for a new rule of faith, but [1] for the comfort of His people, and [2] to correct those who err from Bible truth"—*Early Writings*, 78.

The prophet's work has always contained both comfort and correction. When encouragement is needed, the Lord has sent it through His prophets. When correction has been called for, prophets have delivered this too.

Ellen White learned early that God expected her to give a "straight testimony." But so often encouragement came right along with the correction. After severely rebuking a girl about her personal problems, she spoke these words: "I do not consider your case hopeless; if I did, my pen would not be tracing these lines" —*Testimonies*, 2:562.

There was always the extended invitation to repent, and the assurance of hope, even in the darkest circumstances. Another time she wrote: "You stamped your life record in heaven with a fearful

My Dear Brother M...

Why Ellen White wrote the letters in *Testimonies for the Church*

PAUL A. GORDON

Pacific Press Publishing Association
Nampa, Idaho
Oshawa, Ontario, Canada

Edited by Jerry D. Thomas
Cover photo by Stan Sinclair
Cover and inside design by Dennis Ferree

Gordon, Paul A., 1930-
    My Dear Brother M . . . : why Ellen White wrote the letters
in Testimonies for the church / Paul A. Gordon.
      p.   cm.
    ISBN 0-8163-1369-5 (alk. paper)
    1. White, Ellen Gould Harmon, 1827-1915. 2. Seventh-day
Adventists—Doctrinal controversial works. I. Title.
BX6193.W5G67 1997
286.7'32—dc20   96-33565
                                               CIP

97 98 99 00 01 • 5 4 3 2 1

Contents

blot. Yet deep humiliation and repentance before God will be acceptable to Him"—ibid., 89.

Testimonies were written without favoritism—to General Conference presidents and housewives; hospital administrators and workers in publishing houses; evangelists and local pastors; the aged and the young; a preacher's wife and a teenage girl. Even Ellen White's family members were not exempt.

The prophet's message is that we are to be the best we can be. We are called to step up to higher ground and purer conduct. We are not to settle for the mediocre. We are sons and daughters of the King, and Jesus promises to give us power to succeed. We can still benefit from what was written to previous generations.

Paul A. Gordon

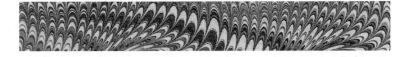

Introduction to Volume 1

1855-1868

This is the volume of beginnings. During the times of this volume, the people later to be known as Seventh-day Adventists tripled their numbers from about 1,500 to 4,500. At the start, there was no name, no organization, no system of financial support, and there were no institutions. At its end, we were called "Seventh-day Adventists" and there were seven conferences organized into a General Conference. We had a plan of finances called "systematic benevolence" that would eventually lead to tithing. We were operating a publishing house and a medical institution. We even had a few permanent church buildings and some elementary schools.

None of these developments came easily. Publishing in our own building began the year this volume began. Choosing a name and organizing a church were strongly resisted by some. Organization was accomplished right in the middle of the American Civil War. Most church enterprises had simple starts. For example, The Western Health Reform Institute—our first medical work—started in 1866 with "two doctors, two bath attendants, one nurse (untrained), three or four helpers, and one patient"—*Medical Missionary*, January 1894.

In 1855, after ten years of Sabbath keeping, we finally settled when to begin and end the Sabbath. At the same time, we also *officially* accepted the prophetic gift among us. Choosing a name would come five years later; organization, three more years down the line.

How can we determine the effect Ellen White's ministry had on the emerging church? Four experiences have been chosen as illustrations.

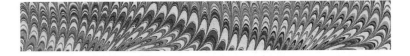

How It All Began

1T 113-115

Nobody likes to be corrected. We don't like it from family, friends, or those with whom we work. It isn't any easier to take from a prophet. In the Old Testament, because kings felt they were responsible only to themselves, prophets had a hard time getting God's messages heard and accepted. Kings seldom welcomed the prophets' claim of higher authority.

When Jesus corrected the Jewish religious leaders, they hated Him, secretly plotting His death all the while. While pledging their confidence in the Old Testament prophets, those leaders resisted when the message came with their names attached.

When the prophetic gift was given to Ellen Harmon at age seventeen, she faced the same resistance. Ignorance of the messenger keeps some from accepting their message. Ironically, a clear understanding of the message also may produce the same resistance because of an unwillingness to do what we know to be right.

But there was much more to Ellen White's call than correction of wrong. Visions contributed to establishing the Seventh-day Adventist Church and its many facets of witness. In November 1848, for example, Ellen White was shown that Adventists should begin to print a paper. The angel told her that from this small beginning it would become "like streams of light that went clear round the world"—*Life Sketches*, 125.

In July 1849, in response to this vision, James White began publishing an eight-page paper, *The Present Truth*. Because Adventists were small in number and scattered widely, for three years the publishing was done wherever the Whites lived, with James as editor. Then, in 1852, a simple hand-operated press was set up in a rented house at Rochester, New York. In 1855, the venture was moved to Battle Creek, Michigan, into a building constructed by Adventists. The last issue of *The Advent Review and Sabbath Herald*, printed in Rochester, appeared on October 30, 1855. For the month of November, publishing was in transit, with the first *Review* coming out on December 4, 1855, at the new location.

That November was a significant month. And this is where our story really begins. Church leaders met at Battle Creek for an urgent discussion of the future of the fledgling church. There was still no formal organization, though publishing had raised interesting questions about the future that must soon be resolved.

Several important topics were discussed at the Battle Creek conference in November 1855. One of these was the relationship the developing church should have to the visions of Ellen White. Note the following sequence of events:

When Christ did not return to earth in 1844, the more than 50,000 waiting Millerites, or Adventists, did not stay together. A small number of about fifty went back to the study of the Bible to see where they had gone wrong in expecting the second advent of Christ at that time. They were scattered across the northeastern United States.

These few Adventists were the nucleus of the Seventh-day Adventist Church. Among them three major developments took place, amazingly enough, all before the year 1844 ended. The seventh-day Sabbath was introduced, a clearer understanding of the heavenly and earthly sanctuary came, and visions were given to 17-year-old Ellen Harmon. How quickly God revealed His interest in the prosperity of His church!

It seemed impossible for these few Adventists to survive as a group. Hardly anyone wanted to listen to their explanation of the sanctuary and the disappointment. The seventh-day Sabbath was certainly not popular. And Ellen Harmon's visions were even more difficult for some to accept. But circumstances began to change, and by 1851, James White could write positively about the future: "Now the door is open almost everywhere to present the truth, and many are prepared to read the publications who have formerly had no interest to investigate"—*The Advent Review and Sabbath Herald*, August 19, 1851 (hereafter identified as the *Review*).

However, as prejudice diminished *outside* the group, James planned a course of action *inside* that in time bore serious consequences. He decided to eliminate all references to Ellen White and her visions in the church paper because some Adventists doubted her prophetic gift. He explained his action in an "Extra" of the *Review*, made up largely of Ellen White's experiences and visions. This "Extra" was to be the first of a paper to be published every two weeks, only for "believers" in Ellen White's visions. He wrote: "As many are prejudiced against visions, we think best at present not to insert anything of the kind in the regular paper. We will therefore publish the visions by themselves for the benefit of those who believe that God can fulfill His word and give visions in the last days"—*Review*, Extra, July 21, 1851.

For more than four years the *Review* was almost silent on Ellen White's work. During these years only five articles by her were published. None referred to visions. This was in startling contrast to what had been done earlier. Interestingly, James White never published another "Extra" as promised. During these four years, the negative treatment of the gift of prophecy, along with the absence of any mention of visions in the columns of the *Review*, led to a general lack of appreciation for the gift.

At the conference called at Battle Creek, in November 1855, it was clear that something was very wrong. A realization of this condition led to "confessions relative to the evident departure of the remnant from the spirit of the message, and the humble, straightforward course taken by those who first embraced it"—*Review*, December 4, 1855.

At about this time, Ellen White wrote: "The visions have been of late less and less frequent, and my testimony for God's people had been gone. I have thought that my work in God's cause was done, and that I had no further duty to do, but to save my own soul, and carefully attend to my little family"—ibid., January 10, 1856.

By 1855 she had published only two small books. One was *Christian Experience and Views of Ellen White* (64 pages), that appeared in 1851. The other was a *Supplement* (48 pages), printed in 1854. These two books, together with the first great controversy account of 1858, today make up the book titled *Early Writings*.

At the November 1855 meeting, Joseph Bates, J.H. Waggoner, and M.E. Cornell were to address the conference regarding spiritual gifts. Here is an excerpt from that statement: "In view of the present low state of the precious cause of our blessed Master, we feel to humble ourselves before God, and confess our unfaithfulness and departure from the way of the Lord . . . . Nor have we appreciated the glorious privilege of claiming the gifts which our blessed Master has vouchsafed to His people; and we greatly fear that we have grieved the Spirit by neglecting the blessings already conferred upon the church . . ."—ibid., December 4, 1855.

The statement then explained their understanding of the proper place of the gift of prophecy: "Nor do we, as some contend, exalt these gifts or their manifestations, above the Bible; on the contrary, we test them by the Bible, making it the great rule of judgment in all things; so that whatever is not in accordance with it, in its spirit and its teachings, we unhesitatingly reject . . ." —ibid.

But then the statement came to a central issue: "While we hold these visions as emanating from the divine Mind, we would confess the inconsistency (which we believe has been displeasing to God) of professedly regarding them as messages from God, and really putting them on a level with the inventions of men. To say that they are of God, and yet we will not be tested by them, is to say that God's will is not a test or rule for Christians"—ibid., December 4, 1855.

On November 20, at the close of the conference, Ellen White was given a vision—the first that she had experienced in nearly three months. "November 20, 1855, while in prayer, the Spirit of the Lord came suddenly and powerfully upon me, and I was taken off in vision. I saw that the Spirit of the Lord has been dying away from the church"—*Testimonies*, 1:113.

The content of this vision was read to the Battle Creek church on November 24, and the thirty-six members voted unanimously to have it published. The initial printing was a two-page broadside. Ellen White then added a few other counsels to complete a small sixteen-page pamphlet, which was published in December 1855, titled *Testimony for the Church*. This was the beginning of the nine volumes we know today as *Testimonies for the Church*.

The conference address at the Battle Creek meeting and Ellen White's subsequent vision marked a turning point for the developing church. It would be eight more years before we would formally organize the General Conference of Seventh-day Adventists. But we were on our way.

Ellen White wrote a few weeks later: "At our late conference in Battle Creek, in November, God wrought for us. The minds of the servants of God were exercised as to the gifts of the Church, and if God's frown had been brought upon His people because the gifts had been slighted and neglected, there was a pleasing prospect that His smiles would again be upon us, and He would graciously and mercifully revive the gifts again, and they would live in the Church, to encourage the desponding and fainting soul, and to correct and reprove the erring"—*Review*, January 10, 1856.

The attitude of those early Adventists toward God's messages made a difference in His continuing to speak through His chosen messenger, Ellen White. Today she no longer lives among us. But the books remain as a testimony to God's leading in the past. But even more than this, they provide encouragement and correction to help us in the present and the future, until Christ returns. We dare not ignore them.

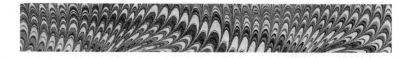

When "Even" Was Not Sunset

1T 116

Ellen White's vision on November 20, 1855, marked the beginning of publishing *Testimonies for the Church*. It contained another very important question—at what time should Sabbath begin? This topic also was discussed at the Battle Creek meeting held November 16-20. It is a story that has some surprises. But first, let's go back about twelve years earlier.

It is the fall of 1843. Eighteen-year-old Delight Oakes had been hired to teach public school at Washington, New Hampshire. Her mother, Rachel Oakes, a Seventh Day Baptist, recently widowed, came to live with her at Washington. The year before, a small church had been built at Washington by the Christian Brethren. But by the time Rachel Oakes and her daughter came to live there, most of the congregation had accepted the second advent preaching of William Miller. Even though Rachel and Delight, as Seventh Day Baptists, observed Sabbath, they attended Sunday services at the church. Frederick Wheeler, a circuit-riding Methodist preacher who also had become a Millerite Adventist, lived in nearby Hillsboro and was the pastor of the Washington church.

One Sunday, probably late in 1843, he conducted a Communion service at Washington. Rachel and Delight were present. Wheeler suggested that only those who kept all of God's commandments should participate. Rachel could hardly keep her seat. After the service, she reminded Wheeler that he was not keeping the seventh-day Sabbath of the fourth commandment. By March 1844, Wheeler was a Sabbath-keeping Adventist minister—the first such anywhere.

T.M. Preble, who lived in nearby Weare, New Hampshire, was pastor of the Free Will Baptist church at Nashua. He also accepted the Sabbath, probably through contact with Wheeler. Preble was the first Adventist to advocate the Sabbath in print in the February 28,1845, issue of *Hope of Israel*, an Adventist periodical published in Portland, Maine. Preble's article and a subsequent tract printed the next month came to the attention of other Adventists. These included fifteen-year-old John Andrews in Paris, Maine, and Joseph Bates in Fairhaven, Massachusetts.

When Joseph Bates, retired sea captain and staunch Adventist, read what Preble had written, he decided to travel to New Hampshire to learn more about the Sabbath for himself. Bates arrived late at night at Wheeler's home in Hillsboro. Never one to be timid about his intentions, he awakened Wheeler, and they studied together the rest of the night. The next day the two of them walked ten miles to Washington, where they met with Cyrus Farnsworth on his front lawn and continued their study. Cyrus and his brother William would be among the first members of the Washington, New Hampshire, church to become Sabbath keepers. Cyrus Farnsworth's brick house still stands today. Delight Oaks would later marry Cyrus. Both she and her mother, Rachel, eventually became Seventh-day Adventists.

Bates was now thoroughly convinced of the truth of the Sabbath. He hurried back to his home in Fairhaven, Massachusetts, with the Sabbath truth burning in his heart. When he met a friend, James Madison Monroe Hall, on the bridge approach between Fairhaven and New Bedford, Hall asked: "Captain Bates, what's the news?"

Bates had an untypical answer: "The news is that the seventh day is the Sabbath."

After they studied together, Hall joined Bates in keeping the next Sabbath.

Joseph Bates wrote a Sabbath tract of his own—*The Sabbath, a Perpetual Sign*—and published it the next year, in August 1846. James and Ellen White were married that same month. They read Bates' tract and accepted the Sabbath. Writing later, Ellen White said: "I believed the truth upon the Sabbath question before I had seen anything in vision in reference to the Sabbath"—Letter 2, 1874.

The next year Ellen White had two visions, about a month apart, regarding the importance of the Sabbath. The first came on March 6, 1847. Bates witnessed this vision at his hometown, Fairhaven, Massachusetts, and published it in a one-page broadside titled, "A Vision." An account of this vision is in *Life Sketches*, 95, 96.

The second vision was given to Ellen White on Sabbath, April 3, 1847, at Topsham, Maine. It first was published as a letter from her to Joseph Bates in his above-mentioned broadside. There are two accounts of this vision, one in *Early Writings*, 32-35, and the other in *Life Sketches*, 100-103.

In both visions she saw heaven's sanctuary and the ark of God in the Most Holy Place. She watched Jesus take the Ten Commandments out of the ark and open them. The fourth commandment shone with a halo of glory around it. By this time there were about fifty Adventists in New England who observed the Sabbath. (See *Testimonies*, 1:77.)

Bates's tract on the Sabbath became the standard work on the subject. There was a major problem, however. Bates, the much-traveled sea captain, knew that sunset occurs at about six p.m. the year-round at the equator. With such knowledge, he believed that each day should begin at that time anywhere in the world. So, in his tract he taught that the Sabbath begins at six p.m. on Friday evening, and ends at six p.m. on Saturday evening. He also used Jesus' parable of the workmen starting at different hours of the day to come to the same conclusion.

Because Bates had introduced the Sabbath to the others, his argument that six p.m. is synonymous with "even," was accepted by many, including James and Ellen White. But there were other Adventists who believed Sabbath began at sunrise. Others believed in sunset time, and still others, midnight. This diversity of practice created some confusion for about ten years.

In June 1854, James White asked Elder D. P. Hall, a minister in Wisconsin (who later defected to the Messenger Party), to write an article on the subject for the *Review*. It was never written. Finally, in the summer of 1855, James asked J. N. Andrews to study the subject. Remember, he was the teenager who read Preble's tract and accepted the Sabbath in Paris, Maine, ten years earlier. James White wrote that Andrews "decided to devote his time to the subject till he ascertained what the Bible taught in regard to it"—*Review*, December 4, 1855.

When the Battle Creek conference was called in November 1855, Andrews' conclusions were presented. (See ibid.) A specific point was made of rejecting the six o'clock time that had been so strongly advocated by Bates. Both Bates and Ellen White hesitated to accept Andrews' conclusions. Then Ellen White was given the vision of November 20. The time to begin the Sabbath was a part of the vision. Her brief account of this part of the vision takes the form of a conversation with an angel: She begins the account by saying: "I saw that it is even so: 'From even to even, shall ye celebrate your Sabbath.' "

Angel: "Take the word of God, read it, understand, and ye cannot err. Read carefully, and ye shall there find what even is, and *when* it is."

Ellen White: "Is the frown of God upon His people for beginning the Sabbath as they have?"

The angel then reviewed the beginnings of the Sabbath among Adventists, and Ellen White did not see that the Lord was displeased.

Ellen White: "Why is it that at this late date we must change the time to begin the Sabbath?"

Angel: "If light come, and that light is set aside or rejected, then comes condemnation and the frown of God; but before the light comes, there is no sin, for there is no light for them to reject"—*Testimonies*, 1:116.

Many Adventists had been under the impression that Ellen White had seen *in vision* that the Sabbath began at six o'clock. But she had only stated that the Sabbath began at "even," and they concluded that "even" was six. The vision ended with Ellen White saying: "The servants of God must draw together, press together."

Later, James White wrote regarding Ellen White's role: "The question naturally rises, If the visions are given to correct the erring, why did she not sooner see the error of the six o'clock time? I have ever been thankful that God corrected the error in His own good time, and did not suffer an unhappy division to exist among us on this point. But, dear reader, the work of the Lord on this point is in perfect harmony with the correct position upon spiritual gifts. It does not appear to be the desire of the Lord to teach His people by the gifts of the Spirit on Bible questions until His servants have diligently searched the word. When this was done on the subject of the time to commence the Sabbath, and most were established, and some were in danger of being out of harmony with the body on this subject, then, yes, *then*, was the very time for God to manifest His goodness in the manifestation of the gifts of His Spirit in the accomplishment of its proper work"—*Review*, February 25, 1868. (Quoted in *Testimonies*, 1:713, 714.)

There are several facts in this story that are interesting to note. The Sabbath was kept in at least four different ways for about ten years among Adventists. Another fact is that Ellen White was a Sunday keeper for almost two years *after* her first vision. And, of course, Ellen White and Joseph Bates were still not thoroughly convinced after Andrews' presentation. A vision corrected them! They accepted the vision as settling the question. And shouldn't this be so? James White had stated the position of the pioneers, that the Bible comes first in understanding truth. Visions brought unity and understanding of the Bible but did not take its place in study to find the truth. It is still the same today.

The First Apostasy

1T 116-118

What is truth? Some truth can be discovered through testing and application. But there is also truth for a certain time. When James White began the publication of our first Adventist periodical in 1849, he called it *The Present Truth*. On the masthead he quoted Peter: "Wherefore I will not be negligent to put you always in remembrance of these things, though ye know them, and be established in the PRESENT TRUTH" (2 Peter 1:12, emphasis was supplied).

In his introduction to this unpretentious eight-page periodical, James White spoke about "truth." "The Church have ever had a present truth. The present truth now, is that which shows present duty, and the right position for us who are about to witness the time of trouble, such as never was. Present truth must be oft repeated, even to those who are established in it. This was needful in the apostles' day, and it certainly is no less important for us, who are living just before the close of time"—*The Present Truth*, July 1849.

But it is not always easy to get a group of people with diverse backgrounds to agree as to what "truth" is. So it was among the small band of Adventists that later was to form the nucleus of the Seventh-day Adventist Church. From the beginning, these Adventists took the Bible as their standard of doctrine. But with so many differing ideas about its meaning, the gift of prophecy through Ellen White and her visions provided stability and unity in understanding of the Scriptures.

There was another major problem that was dealt with at the November 1855 meeting. This story also needs to be told.

It had to do with the first apostasy among Adventists, known as the "Messenger party" and its magazine, *The Messenger of Truth*. But *truth* it was not. Its beginning goes back to the time James and Ellen White visited the Adventist church in Jackson, Michigan, in June 1854.

Ellen White had seen in vision that the church was in confusion. She spoke to them about what she had been shown regarding one woman in particular. Two ministers there, H. S. Case and C. P. Russell, were, in Ellen White's words, "greatly prejudiced against this sister, and cried out, 'Amen! Amen!' and manifested a spirit of triumph over her, and would frequently say, 'I thought so! It is just so!' "—*Spiritual Gifts*, 2:181.

Ellen White was so "distressed" at their attitude, that she sat down before she finished relating her whole vision. Case and Russell "exhorted others to receive the vision, and manifested such a spirit that my husband reproved them," said Ellen White. The meeting ended in further confusion.

That night, Ellen White received another vision. The part of the vision that she had not revealed, was repeated to her. She was shown the wrong attitude of Case and Russell. She saw they were a major cause of division because of their proud attitude. She wrote: "I saw why the Lord had hid from me the part of the vision that related to them. It was that they might have opportunity to manifest before all what spirit they were of"—ibid.

Another meeting was called the next day, where she shared what she had seen the night before in vision. But these men, who earlier had strongly supported the visions, did not accept her rebuke of them. They fought against her message, and shortly after, began what was to be known as the Messenger party. In September 1854, they began to publish their paper, *The Messenger of Truth*.

At about this time J. M. Stephenson and D. P. Hall, recent converts, began to preach for the Adventists in Wisconsin. These two men, however, had accepted the "age to come" theory of the millennium. This theory held that the second advent of Christ would mark the beginning of one thousand years where probation would continue and the nations would be converted under the reign of Christ and His saints. They taught that the Jews were also to play a key role.

Some former Millerite preachers had also accepted this theory after the disappointment. These included Joseph Marsh, who published a pamphlet entitled *"Age to Come,"* and also edited *The Advent Harbinger*. His assistant on the journal was none other than O. R. L. Crosier, who had studied with Hiram Edson and had written an article for the *Day Star Extra*, February 7, 1846, that had helped to provide a correct understanding of the sanctuary and the disappointment. It had been endorsed by Ellen White as in harmony with what she had seen in vision. (See *A Word to the Little Flock*, 12). But Crosier had left the Sabbath-keeping Adventists over the Sabbath doctrine. However, he remained with a branch of the Sunday-keeping Adventists.

The larger group of Adventists under the leadership of Joshua Himes, had rejected the "age to come" theory after 1844. The small group that would eventually become the Seventh-day Adventist Church also rejected it.

In June 1854, James and Ellen White visited both Case and Russell in Jackson, Michigan, and Stephenson and Hall in Wisconsin. James told of conversation with them: "When we were in Eldorado, Wisconsin, June 1854, Elders Stephenson and Hall stated to us that they were firm believers in the 'age to come.' We asked them if they had ever known one sinner converted, or a backslider reclaimed, as the fruits of preaching 'age to come.' The answer was 'No.' We inquired, 'Then why preach it?' "

A pertinent question that might be asked of others, even today, who would preach a false message.

James continues the account: "The reply was 'We are willing to waive the subject, and unite on the third angel's message, if those who oppose the age to come will do the same.' We then stated that we could speak in behalf of brethren [in the] East, that they would be willing to waive the subject"—*Review*, December 4, 1855.

James White then invited them to come east to preach. It was at this time that he asked Hall to write an article for the *Review* on the correct time to begin the Sabbath. Hall never wrote the article.

In 1855, Stephenson and Hall attended a conference in Jackson, Michigan, and participated in meetings at Mill Grove and Rochester, New York. While they were in Rochester, James White took them into confidence about the work at the publishing office. Ellen White writes about it: "While my husband was openhearted and unsuspecting, seeking ways to remove their jealousy, and frankly opening to them the affairs of the office, and trying to help them, they were watching for evil, and observing everything with a jealous eye"—*Testimonies*, 1:117.

As plans were being made for the transfer of the publishing work from Rochester to Battle Creek, in November 1855, Stephenson and Hall returned to Wisconsin. They began to openly oppose the *Review* and James White, and turned to their own publication. Ellen White speaks about them: "I was shown the case of Stephenson and Hall of Wisconsin. I saw that while we were in Wisconsin, in June 1854, they were convicted that the visions were of God, but they examined them and compared them with their views of the 'age to come,' and because the visions did not agree with these, they sacrificed the visions for the 'age to come.' And while on their journey east last spring, they were both wrong and designing."

She then spoke of their joining with the Messenger party: "These men are uniting with a lying and corrupt people. They have evidence of this. And while they were professing sympathy and union with my husband, they (especially Stephenson) were biting like an adder behind his back"—ibid.

At the same time that James and Ellen White were dealing with the Messenger party, they had several personal challenges. Anna, James's sister, was dying of tuberculosis. Luman Masten, at the printing office in Rochester, was also dying of the same disease. And James White, himself, was in very poor health. If this were not enough, Ellen gave birth to her third son, William, on August 29, 1854.

But the health of James presents another side to the story. Ellen White writes of it: "The '*Messenger*' party, the most of whom had been reproved through visions for their wrongs, framed all manner of falsehoods concerning us, and concerning the visions. Some of the writers of the '*Messenger*' even triumphed over the feebleness of my husband, saying, that God will take care of him, and remove him out of the way. Faith revived, and my husband exclaimed, 'I shall not die, but live and declare the works of the Lord, and may yet preach their funeral sermon' "—*Spiritual Gifts*, 2:195, 196.

It may seem surprising, but Ellen White seemed to welcome the formation of the Messenger party. When they separated from the church in 1855, she saw in vision that their leaving was a blessing. With a certain sense of relief, she wrote: "God's frown has been brought upon the church on account of individuals with corrupt hearts being in it. They have wanted to be foremost, when neither God not their brethren placed them there. Selfishness and exaltation have marked their course."

Then, speaking of the forming of the Messenger party, she perhaps smiled as she said: "A place is now open for all such where they can go and find pasture with those of their kind"—*Testimonies*, 1:122.

There was little opposition from the secular world then. The established churches sometimes caused problems. Some of the most bitter opposition came from their former friends in the Advent faith—"first-day Adventists." But James White pointed out what was even worse: "Those trials which arise among ourselves are the most severe"—*Review*, September 5, 1854.

White then said: "It is not our duty to leave the work of God to contend with unreasonable men. It is our duty to point out and warn the flock to beware of the influence of those who cause divisions, then leave the matter in the hands of God"—ibid.

In June 1855, Ellen White was shown the same thing in vision: "I saw that the people of God must arouse and put on the armor. Christ is coming, and the great work of the last message of mercy is of too much importance for us to leave it and come down to answer such falsehoods, misrepresentations, and slanders as the *Messenger* party have fed upon and have scattered abroad"—*Testimonies*, 1:123.

Ellen White saw in vision that though some honest people had been misled by the Messenger party, a change was coming: "I saw that such will have evidence of the truth of these matters. The church of God should move straight along, as though there were not such a people in the world"—ibid.,117.

Those who gathered at the November 1855 conference at Battle Creek obviously agreed with James and Ellen White. They went on record as follows:

"*Whereas*, Inquiries have been made as to what course we designed to pursue in the future, in reference to the misstatements of the enemies of present truth, therefore, for the information and satisfaction of the brethren abroad.

"*Resolved*, That we henceforth devote ourselves exclusively to the advocacy and defense of the present truth, conducting ourselves in all things to Him who judgeth righteously, after the example of our Pattern, in affliction and in patience"—*Review*, December 4, 1855.

We can still apply this principle today!

Within three years, the Messenger party had all but disappeared. What happened to them? James White tells about a few of their leaders: "Wyman, rejected by his party for crime, and a town charge. Bezzo, their editor [turned schoolteacher], fined $25 for presenting a pistol, and threatening to shoot a scholar in school. Case, run out as a preacher, and fishing on the lakes. Chapin, in a clothing store. Lillis, a spiritualist. Russell and Hicks had denounced Bezzo and the publishers of their sheet [as] hypocrites, and were standing alone"—*Review*, January 14, 1858.

What about Stephenson and Hall in Wisconsin? Stephenson adopted views that cut him off from the others and he divorced his wife to marry a younger woman. J. N. Loughborough reported: "In this forlorn condition—friendless, penniless, and with failing health—he was placed in the 'poorhouse.' There his mental faculties failed him—not a derangement, but a state of imbecility. The last four years of his life he had no more sense, or ability to care for himself, than a year-old child"—*Pacific Union Recorder*, May 12, 1910.

D. P. Hall stopped preaching, and went into selling real estate. He later went bankrupt. This led to discouragement and finally, insanity. And so the first apostasy was ended among Adventists though a few from this group later joined with others to form the Church of God (Adventist).

Ellen White wrote later about such apostasies: "Satan knows how to make his attacks. He works upon minds to excite jealousy and dissatisfaction toward those at the head of the work. The gifts are next questioned; then, of course, they have but little weight, and instruction given through vision is disregarded. Next follows skepticism in regard to the vital points of our faith, the pillars of our position, then doubt as to the Holy Scriptures, and then the downward march to perdition. When the *Testimonies*, which were once believed, are doubted and given up, Satan knows the deceived ones will not stop at this; and he redoubles his efforts till he launches them into open rebellion, which becomes incurable, and ends in destruction"—*Testimonies*, 5:672.

What an accurate prediction! Will there be apostasy in the future? It is likely. But just as surely, God will continue to take care of His church.

"The Nameless One"

1T 223, 224

On the surface, it would seem a simple thing to choose a name, whether of an organization or of a newborn baby. But it was not easy in either case in early Adventist history. Sometimes names are labels that are used to ridicule. Religious groups often have the same trouble with names that individuals do. What comes to mind when you hear the name "Methodist"? "Quaker"? "Shaker"? "Millerite"? These are labels that originally were attached by enemies.

But there is sometimes as much of a problem when a group sets out to name itself. The name "Seventh-day Adventist" did not come easily. Sentiment among Adventists ran very strongly against choosing a name—any name. But a change was coming. The day before Christmas, 1850, Ellen White received a vision. She wrote: "I saw everything in heaven was in perfect order . . . Said the angel, 'Behold ye and know how perfect, how beautiful, the order in heaven. Follow it' "—MS 11, 1850. (See *Messenger to the Remnant*, 45.)

The Millerite movement, from which our pioneers had come, had not taken kindly to organization, or choosing a name. The following is taken from the leading Millerite paper: "Take care that you do not seek to organize another church. No church can be organized by a man's invention but what it becomes Babylon the moment it is organized"—*The Midnight Cry*, February 15, 1844.

George Storrs, the author of these words, was a leading advocate of the October 22 date for Christ's second coming. It is perhaps ironic that he was one of the first Millerite preachers to leave the movement after the disappointment, calling it a delusion.

The decade from 1850 to 1860 marked a steady development of order among our early Adventist pioneers. The first deacons were chosen, discipline was administered, the first Sabbath-School lessons were written, cards of recommendation for ministers were signed by James White and Joseph Bates, meetinghouses were erected, tents were used for evangelistic meetings, and "systematic benevolence" was begun.

All of these developments still had not brought about full organization of the church. Here is where the publishing work comes into the story. For the first eleven years of Adventist publishing, its business success or failure rested almost entirely on James White. Adventists frequently invested their money with hope of a profit. This "borrowed money" was the subject of three paragraphs by James White in the *Review* of February 23, 1860. He said that borrowed money he had received for publishing was not secure, and hinted that a recognized church should be operating the venture.

Roswell F. Cottrell, a leading Adventist minister, responded: "For myself I think it would be wrong to 'make us a name,' since that lies at the foundation of Babylon" —*Review*, March 22, 1860.

There's that word "Babylon" again. He then made the following point: "I think it is for us to take the best care of the property we can and then trust it with the Lord. . . Those that lend money to the office, lend it to the Lord and they must trust the Lord for it"—ibid.

James White replied immediately in an editorial:

1. "Babylon signifies confusion, and refers to the confusion of languages of the Babel-builders, and not to their making themselves a name."

2. "If wrong to hold church property legally, how can it be

right for individual members to hold property legally?"

3. "To send out a few hundred dollars worth of books [Cottrell's suggestion] would not obviate a twentieth part of the difficulty. If we should leave this matter with the Lord, as Brother R.F.C. says, why not leave the books in his hands at the Office with the other property?"

James White argued that those who had invested money in the publishing venture might want it back, forcing the closing of the publishing office. Then, he came directly to Cottrell's major point: " 'Leave this matter to the Lord.' This is the plea. Well, if the Lord has not left the management of his goods to us, that with them we may spread the truth, then we can leave it with him. But we regard it dangerous to leave with the Lord what he has left with us, and thus sit down upon the stool of do little, or nothing."

White went on: "Now it is perfectly right to leave the sun, moon and stars with the Lord; also the earth with its revolutions, the ebbing and flowing of the tides, the running of the rivers, the changing seasons, sunshine and rain, heat and cold—we say, 'Let us leave these with the Lord.' But if God in his everlasting word calls on us to act the part of faithful stewards of his goods, we had better attend to these matters in a legal manner—the only way we can handle real estate in this world"—ibid., April 5, 1860.

This marked the beginning of a prolonged debate in the *Review* on organization. This finally led to the calling of a meeting at Battle Creek on September 29, 1860. Churches were asked to appoint delegates. Arrangements were announced:

"Several empty houses will be engaged for the use of those who come in campmeeting style. . . . Also stables and barns will be hired for horses. Stable room and hay for horses will be provided for 50 cents each, for three nights"—ibid., September 4, 1860.

The second notice gave more details of the purpose for the meeting: "The principle object of this general gathering is to call . . . active friends of the cause, to consider several important questions, such as the proper method of holding church property, the wants of our Office of publication, etc."—ibid., September 11, 1860.

Those who came were not a group of gray-haired brethren. It's true that Joseph Bates, sixty-eight years old, was selected as chairman. That was expected. But among those gathered were James White, thirty-nine; Ellen White, thirty-two; Uriah Smith, twenty-eight; J. N. Andrews, thirty-one; J. H. Waggoner, forty; M. E. Cornell, thirty-three; and J. N. Loughborough, twenty-eight.

An evidence of the importance of the meeting is that the minutes filled several pages of the October 9, 16, and 23 issues of the *Review*. At the meetings, Moses Hull (who later became a leading spiritualist) moved that because James White had written so much on the subject of organization, he should present his views.

James White then spoke of the problems that Cottrell's opposition had created. Cottrell was not there, but had written a letter stating his views, and it was read. This prompted considerable discussion over a period of three days, becoming especially heated when the topic turned to choosing a name. T. J. Butler, the delegate from Gilboa, Ohio, strongly favored the name "Church of God." James White had also favored such a name earlier.

It was made clear that if we were to organize our publishing work, the church that would own it needed a name. When the morning meeting adjourned on Sunday, September 30, a committee consisting of Andrews, Waggoner and Butler was appointed to provide a suggestion for a name. When they again convened at four p.m., the committee had no recommendation. That afternoon, the "Advent Review Publishing Association" was formed. But still no name for the church.

On Monday morning, October 1, a constitution was presented and approved for the publishing association. It was then moved that we adopt a name for the church. There was more discussion regarding choosing a church name. Brother Butler, from Ohio, again proposed the name "Church of God." More discussion. At eleven a.m., it was voted to adjourn for one hour.

When they reconvened, the question of choosing a name was once again taken up, and a vote was taken to adopt a name. The account states: "The name Church of God was proposed and zealously advocated by some [no doubt by T. J. Butler from Ohio]. It was objected that this name was already in use by some denominations, and on that account, was indefinite, besides having to the world an appearance of presumption"—ibid., October 23, 1860.

Finally the name "Seventh-day Adventist" was proposed as a name that would be "expressive of our faith and position." Brother Hewitt offered the following: "Resolved, That we take the name Seventh-day Adventists." For some reason, the group did not like the wording, and the following was suggested by Brother Poole: "Resolved, That we call ourselves Seventh-day Adventists."

After lengthy consideration, the resolution was passed, with only Brother Butler dissenting and four others not voting. Moses Hull then moved that the name chosen be recommended to the churches generally. This was passed, again, with Brother Butler the only one voting against the resolution. T. J. Butler, by the way, later created other problems in Ohio and left the church.

Ellen White's vision regarding the name, first published in *Testimony for the Church*, number 6, in January, 1861, is better understood in light of the 1860 meeting just considered. She said: "The name Seventh-day Adventist carries the true features of our faith in front, and will convict the inquiring mind. . . . I was shown that almost every fanatic who has arisen who wishes to hide his sentiments that he may lead away others, claims to belong to *the church of God*. . . . The name is too indefinite for the remnant people of God"—*Testimonies*, 1:224 (emphasis supplied).

Soon after the conference, Roswell F. Cottrell accepted the action and wrote an apology: "If any have been encouraged in a spirit of waywardness by what I have written, I am sorry for it. I did not intend it. And I would exhort such to put away such a spirit, to seek pardon for the past, and in the future endeavor to keep the unity of the Spirit in the bond of peace"—*Review*, November 6, 1860.

So, the name of the church had been chosen. But there was still another name to choose. James and Ellen White's fourth son was born on September 20, just nine days before this historic meeting at Battle Creek. With three sons already, the Whites were perhaps caught off guard. Maybe they hoped for a daughter this time.

Or they might have been so busy planning for the meeting that there had been no time to decide on a name. Whatever the reason, when he was born, they had no name chosen.

Immediately after the meeting James was called to travel to Illinois and Wisconsin. Seven letters are preserved from Ellen White to her husband between October 12 and November 21, 1860. Here are some excerpts:

"Our *nameless one* grows finely, weighed him last Wednesday. He then weighed ten pounds and one quarter. He is well"—October 12 (Letter 10, 1860).

"The little *nameless one* was weighed this morning. He weighed eleven pounds and three quarters. He is quite good-natured"—Early October (Letter 12a, 1860).

"The little *nameless one* is fat and rugged, and very quiet, has not had a cold yet"—October 22 (Letter 11, 1860).

In other letters she refers to him as "babe" and "the fourth one."

Letters to Lucinda Hall, a close friend, finds Ellen White using familiar words again:

"We have just weighed our *nameless one*"—October 24 (Letter 17, 1860).

Still another to Lucinda:

"I improve this opportunity while the yet *nameless one* is asleep. (Send him a name)"—November 2 (Letter 18, 1860, all emphasis supplied).

On November 16, James was visiting in Markesan, Wisconsin, and had what he called a "presentiment" that the baby was very sick. He saw the baby lying in Ellen's lap, with his head and face terribly swollen. James wrote to her, telling her of what he had seen. When she received the letter on November 19, the baby was perfectly well. That night, however, the bed was made with damp sheets, and the next morning he was very sick, with symptoms to those James had witnessed.

The same night he had "seen" his sick son, James dreamed that a certain firm of brokers in Battle Creek were selling shopworn shoes in a small store. This seemed strange to him, and he awoke wondering if the dream had any significance.

Earlier, because there was no bank in Battle Creek at that time, James had deposited with this seemingly reliable firm, $1,800 that had been sent to him to be invested in stock for the publishing association. Memories of his dream left him until, a few days later when he received a telegram from Ellen. She had written: "Monday night [November 19] our child was taken sick in the night and all day yesterday was very sick, dangerous. . . . He is a very sick child. I thought you had ought to know this, and then you could do as you pleased about returning"—Letter 15, 1860.

James *did* return home on November 25, in time to see his son before he died on December 14, 1860, after living less than three months. The Whites had finally named their son, John Herbert. With no other preacher available, James spoke at his own son's funeral. The afternoon of the same day, as he was entering the *Review* office, he remembered the other part of his dream, that seemed to indicate that the money in the hands of the brokers was not safe. He called the office workers together and told them that he believed God was warning him. A decision was made to immediately invest the money in building materials for the new office. By the last of June, all the money had been withdrawn from the brokers. Two days later they were declared bankrupt. Other depositors in Battle Creek lost more than $50,000.

Many knew that James had invested money with these men, and asked: "How much did you lose by these men?" James White could answer: "Not one dollar." The experience had far-reaching influence as others heard of it, and many invested money with the *Review* office without interest, knowing that God would protect it—*Life Sketches* (1880 edition), 351-353.

John Herbert, James and Ellen White's fourth son, never saw his first birthday. But the church named that year has grown from barely fifty hearty souls after the disappointment, to several million worldwide. Can it be that just as publishing interests helped us toward a name, so publishing around the world will help to finish the work so nobly begun? Surely it will.

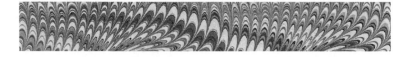

Introduction to Volume 2

1868-1871

The prophetic gift is, without doubt, the most difficult gift to use. First, you don't decide to *be* a prophet. Second, you don't decide the *content* of a vision. Third, you don't even decide *when* to have a vision. All of these decisions come from God. Then, if you add the element of the seemingly impossible—like Noah's message that there is to be rain, or Elijah's message that there is to be no rain for several years, you realize that a prophet is in a hard place.

But there are still other problems for the prophet. Like revealing the secret sins of people. Or giving a king a message from a higher Authority. To better understand this difficulty, we must remember that kings were above challenge by any of their subjects—or so they thought. It was Jeremiah who was encouraged not to be "afraid of their faces." Jonah ran in the opposite direction, when he was asked to warn Ninevah. And Ellen Harmon, at age seventeen, "begged the Lord to give the work to someone else."

From a present perspective, it might be easy for us to accept that prophets would quite naturally take on a correcting role given by the Lord. But none of us like to be corrected. It may be that we are too proud. It may be that we feel that our information or skills are better than the one who corrects us. It may be that we want to be independent from all external authority. But whatever the reason, we cannot avoid our responsibility and dependence upon God.

This volume of the *Testimonies* deals with personal messages. We will review just two: The first to her son, Edson, and the other to a girl whose name we do not know.

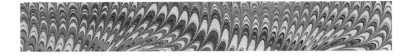

"Dear Son"

2T 261-268

Why did Ellen White choose to publish a letter she had written to her son, Edson, on his nineteenth birthday? Maybe she wanted to remind the church that even her own family was not free from the need of God's saving grace. It is not easy to be a prophet's son—so much is expected of him. It would be the natural thing to resent the fact that life seems to be lived under the microscope. Every son or daughter of a public person can identify with Edson.

As part of maturing, every young person needs to establish an identity. Some choose to honor their parents and their God by word and action and some do not. James and Ellen White had four sons. Their oldest, Henry, died of pneumonia at age sixteen. The last son, John Herbert, lived only three months, dying of a brain infection. The two remaining sons, Edson and Willie, did not have an easy life in the early years as their parents traveled extensively. Ellen White would have preferred to be at home with her family. She once wrote: "Although the cares that came upon us in connection with the publishing work and other branches of the cause involved much perplexity, the greatest sacrifice which I was called to make in connection with the work was to leave my children frequently to the care of others"—*Life Sketches*, 165.

She went on to say: "I was often grieved as I thought of the contrast between my situation and that of others who . . . could ever be with their children, to counsel and instruct them"—ibid.

Both Edson and Willie had several periods of time when their parents were away from home, putting them under "the care of others." Their parents wrote to them—letters of news, but also of counsel. Ellen White's letter on Edson's nineteenth birthday was one such letter. It suggests that all was not well with him.

She speaks of his "waywardness" (261). "It is not natural for you to love spiritual things" (263). "Every day increases your distance from God" (267, 268).

Along with these cautions, she encourages Edson to seek a higher level of Christianity. She says: "Aim to honor God in everything. . . . Be thorough in whatever you undertake." "You should be in earnest to obtain an experience in the Christian life" (262).

In this letter we find a most positive encouragement to commit ourselves to the Lord: "By what means shall we determine whose side we are on? Who has the heart? With whom are our thoughts? Upon whom do we love to converse? Who has our warmest affections and our best energies? If we are on the Lord's side, our thoughts are with Him, and our sweetest thoughts are of Him" (262).

Edson was born in July 1849, the month that his father published the first *Present Truth*. When he was nine-months-old he was left for five weeks in the care of Clarissa Bonfoey, whose parent had recently died. Ellen White speaks of her return to a sick son: "We found Sister Bonfoey and little Edson. The child was very feeble . . . We prayed for the child, and his symptoms became more favorable, and we journeyed with him to Oswego (New York) to attend a conference there"—*Life Sketches*, 135. After several weeks, he recovered. But again, his parents had to leave him with others so that they could meet appointments in the field.

When Edson was three, they lived in Rochester, New York. A cholera epidemic raged through the city. Ellen White spoke of "carriages bearing the dead . . . rumbling through the streets. . . . At almost every corner," she said, "we would meet wagons with plain pine coffins in which to put the dead"—ibid.,143.

Then Edson became sick with cholera. For three days he ate nothing. The Whites had speaking appointments for two months. They were to travel by horse and carriage and they hardly dared to leave until they had some positive sign that Edson was better. They prayed that if he would have an appetite, they would go. Two days later, at about noon, he asked for food. They began their trip that very afternoon—*with Edson in the carriage* on his mother's lap. After the long vigil she had maintained at his bedside, Ellen White kept dropping off to sleep, and Edson would begin to slip off her lap. Finally she tied him on her lap and they proceeded. Their faith was rewarded and at the end of the trip, their son was well again.

As a youth in his teens, Edson showed skills in music, business, editing, and printing. At age fifteen, he was employed at the *Review* office in Battle Creek and very quickly became a master printer. It was at this time, however, that his mother wrote to him: "I understand your dangers and your temptations as few parents can, for He who understandeth the secrets of the heart has been pleased to show me your peculiar dangers and besetments."

She went on: "Your parents, who live for you and are desirous of your present and future happiness, see you taking a course which leads them often to doubt what you say and to look upon you distrustingly because they know that you are often planning and entering into schemes and enterprises and concealing it from those who gave you birth."

We hear her crying as she writes: "Dear Edson, permit your own deep-feeling tender-hearted mother to appeal to you while her tears cannot be restrained."

Then, she comes to the hardest part: "O, Edson, it is the knowledge of these things that is wearing me out and bringing upon me discouragement which will compel me to cease laboring in the cause of God"—Letter 4, 1865. (Quoted in *Manuscript Releases*, 4:173-177.)

Many parents can identify with such words!

Edson grew to adult life and married. For three years in the

1880s, he managed Pacific Press at Oakland, California. But then he went into private publishing and drifted from the church. When some personal business dealings with the church did not go well, the experience embittered him, even against his own mother.

In 1893, Edson was in Chicago, in debt and discouraged. He was now forty-four years of age. Ellen White was in Australia. An exchange of letters between Edson and her reveals serious problems. Sending a handwritten letter to him on April 18, she expressed her fears: "It seems at times more than I can bear that the world should find in any child of mine, countenance to the forgetting of God . . . If one who has had so large light will let himself down into Satan's service, Satan will make the most of him through his influence to make the truth of God a lie. . . .

"It is not yet too late for wrongs to be righted, but if the devil can by his devices snatch you away from this life while you are in rebellion against God, then hell will triumph. Shall it be? . . . Oh, be converted, soul and body and spirit."

Ellen White closes the letter with these words to his wife: "Daughter Emma, I send this to your address for I know not as Edson will receive it or even read it. Mother"—Letter 116, 1893.

A month later, on May 18, Edson replies, in a letter full of bitterness: "I am more sorry than I can say for the series of circumstances which cut me off from you and W.C. (Willie, his brother). But when I was refused any kind of redress from the demoniacal course pursued towards me by those representing you in connection with my business, I then and there decided that never would I again communicate until the matter was righted."

Later in the letter, he says: "I have no religious inclinations in the least . . . I am not a Christian yet." He then speaks of money owed him, and resentment that it has not been paid: "I ask that orders be given the postmaster at Battle Creek to deliver the Central Manufacturing Company's mail to me. There is nothing in it worth while, but you can show me that much consideration. Then, there are from $150 to $200 on the books that could have been collected if any effort had been made to do so. I could have assisted them to collect, but they took matters into their own hands—made no effort to collect, and were too high and mighty to consult me in the matter." Edson letter, May 18, 1893.

In her next letter to Edson, dated June 21, Ellen White does not make excuses for how he has been treated. Instead, she expresses disappointment at the direction his life is taking: "Why should you express yourself as you have done? Why use such firm language? Why do you have any satisfaction in this selfish independence?"

She continues: "You feel we have cut ourselves loose from you but if you could only know how much we studied how to hold fast to you and have the approval of God, and not serve with your wrong course of action, you would pity us, for we have had soul agony and sent up our prayers to God with many tears."

Then Ellen White speaks of a dream in which she sees Edson and four other young men on a beach. They are careless and unconcerned about a severe undertow and ignore warnings to stay out of the water. All are drowned but one. She awakes as Edson is caught in the waves. It is not clear if he is the one who is saved.

She writes: " 'Not at all religiously inclined.' These are the words of Satan, not of my son . . . What record does this bear to the world? I cannot say now, as one expressed in a letter to me not long since, 'If my children are not saved, I do not care to be saved and know they perish.' No! No! I have seen the happiness and joy and glory of the blessed . . . I shall not but go with remorse to the grave that it may be my best efforts in behalf of my own son have been as naught; that I should be brought to reproach and be a byword to my enemies and to apostates, to evil angels, and to men."

Sober words from a grieving mother. Then she pleads: "You can in the strength of Jesus change this order of things. You can now, while it is called today, harden not your heart."

Later in the letter she speaks plainly again: "I have been made to feel there is a sorrow deeper than bereavement by death. It is breaches in affection—the closest ties rudely sundered and those who have done everything they could do in your behalf treated as your enemies, your love turned to hatred, the door of the heart rudely closed against those who have made your interest their own and lavished upon you every kindness in thought and in affections."

She ends her letter, however, with these positive words: "I cannot save you; God alone can save you. But work, while Jesus invites you, in harmony with God. Mother"—Letter 123, 1893.

Edson's next letter to his mother, on August 10, shows a marked change in attitude. Obviously, the work of conversion had begun. He writes: "I have surrendered fully and completely, and never enjoyed life before as I am now. I have for years been under a strain, with so much to accomplish, and it has stood right in my way. Now, I have left it all with my Saviour, and the burden does not bear me down any longer."

He continues: "I certainly am very sorry that I have been such a burden of care to you, and hope I shall not be any longer. I want to connect with the work of the cause in some way as soon as possible." Edson letter, August 10, 1893.

Two months later, in October, 1893, Edson heard a presentation on work for Blacks in the southern United States and felt drawn to such work. Edson found a tract his mother had published in 1891, speaking about the South. It said: "White men and white women should be qualifying themselves to work among the colored people . . . The black man's name is written in the book of life beside the white man's. All are one in Christ" (see *The Southern Work*, 9-18).

In January 1894, Edson and Will Palmer, a friend from earlier years, attended meetings in Atlanta, Georgia, dealing with the work in the southern states. An idea came to build a boat. A boat builder was hired in Battle Creek, and five months later, in July, the boat—*The Morning Star*—was launched.

Over the next few years, Edson worked successfully in the South in extremely dangerous circumstances. Edson's new-found religious experience was to be tested again and again, both by the work, and by the attitudes of some church leaders in Battle Creek. But with a growing faith and the encouragement of his mother, both in money and counsel, he had a lasting impact on the work that can still be felt today. On March 7, 1897, it was voted that Edson should be ordained.

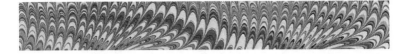

"You Are Not Hopeless"

2T 558-565

While Ellen White's call to prophetic work included giving comfort to those who were discouraged, she was frequently required to give strong messages of correction. But note an unusual statement: "God loves His people who keep His commandments, and reproves them, not because they are the worst, but because they are the best people in the world"—*Testimonies*, 1:569.

Does that surprise you? It shouldn't, really. God has sent correction, both in Bible times, and in more modern times, because He loves us. And the *Testimonies* contain some pretty tough messages.

In the first few pages of volume 2, Ellen White recalls an eastern tour of the United States in 1868, where she gave several personal messages to people. Many of these people wrote to her afterward, requesting that she write out what she had spoken to them. The responsibility for writing seemed to overwhelm Ellen White, and she actually became sick for several days. She questioned whether it was her duty to write so much—and to some who seemed to be unworthy or not interested.

In this state of mind, Ellen White had a dream. In the dream a person brought her some white cloth and asked her to cut out garments "for persons of all sizes and all descriptions of character and circumstances in life." These garments were to be hung up, ready to be finished when called for. As she cut out garments, she wondered if there was to be an end to her work. But more were waiting to be cut out.

She expressed discouragement at the amount of work ahead of her. For more than twenty years she had done this work, and it seemed that her efforts had gone unappreciated, and had not seemed to accomplish much good. It was obvious that the "garments" in her dream represented messages she was giving to people.

When she asked about one woman who didn't appreciate her garment, the person in the dream replied: "Cut out the garments. That is your duty. The loss is not yours, but mine. God sees not as man sees. He lays out the work that He would have done, and you do not know which will prosper, this or that. It will be found that many such poor souls will go into the kingdom, while others, who are favored with all the blessings of life, having good intellects and pleasant surroundings, giving them all the advantages of improvement, will be left out"—ibid., 2:11.

Obviously, Christ was the Person in the dream. His words remind us all that we are to leave results in His hands. In the dream, Ellen White held up her calloused hands and wished she could stop her work. But she was told: "Cut out the garments. Your release has not yet come." Wearily, she stood up to go back to her work. Then, she saw a new pair of scissors. She picked them up and began to cut. Her weariness left her, and she was able to cut out many garments with little effort.

After this dream, the Whites and J. N. Andrews began a trip through Michigan. She was further encouraged by the positive responses she received in many places, especially from one family, to whom she had written "very pointed testimony"—ibid., 10-12.

A few months later, on June 12, 1868, she received a vision

while preaching in Battle Creek, telling her to publish testimonies for all to read. She wrote: "When the Lord singles out individual cases and specifies their wrongs, others, who have not been shown in vision, frequently take it for granted that they are right, or nearly so. If one is reproved for a special wrong, brethren and sisters should carefully examine themselves to see wherein they have failed and wherein they have been guilty of the same sin"—ibid., 122.

This all brings us to one of the strongest letters Ellen White ever wrote. And it was to a single girl, probably in her mid-teens. The letter can be divided into two parts. The first might be titled, "What you are," and the second, "What you can become." And there are two sentences separating these two parts, that say: "I do not consider your case hopeless; if I did, my pen would not be tracing these lines. In the strength of God you can redeem the past"—ibid., 562.

We do not know who this girl was. What would you have done if you had received such a letter? I hope the girl read both parts. It is important for us, even today, to read both parts. There were a lot of things wrong in this teenage girl's life. Her parents had indulged her whims. They had believed her stories against her teacher. They had pampered her at home, not requiring her to work. She was addicted to fictional love stories. She never read the Bible. She had no serious thought about her Christian life. Boys dominated most of her waking thoughts.

To get the full impact of what she wrote, let's use Ellen White's words, as she described the girl's character: Proud, vain, headstrong, willful, stubborn, deceptive, troublesome, impudent, defiant, lack modesty, bold, selfish, self-exalted, impure mind, corrupt imagination, a bitter spirit, an evil influence, a violated conscience, daydreamer, unsanctified feelings, independent spirit, wayward, daring, base passion controls, forward with the boys, almost a fool, a deceitful tongue.

And there were still more descriptive terms. What a list! How would you feel if you received such a letter? Too harsh? No. This girl needed what we all need—a thorough conversion. And that's what the last part of the letter is all about.

Parents, teachers, and, especially, God Himself want the best for us. The Lord says to the end-time church, Laodicea: "As many as I love, I rebuke and chasten: be zealous, therefore, and repent" (see Revelation 3:19).

God points out our sins, and then offers hope and forgiveness. Jesus did it for the woman taken in adultery, when He said to her: "Neither do I condemn thee: go and sin no more" (see John 8:10).

And that brings us to the last half of the letter to this girl. After saying there is hope, Ellen White encourages her to change. Notice how often words are used that are nearly opposite to the earlier correction. These are again the exact words of the letter: You can change, use powers God has given you, gain a moral excellence, you can be elevated, come to God, awaken your conscience, cherish God's presence, you can be a blessing to your parents, an instrument of righteousness to your associates, you can be a partaker of the divine nature, you can bless your sisters, read the Bible, be guided by its teachings, have more experience before marriage, guard your thoughts, passions and affections, devote your affections to God, you can become prudent, modest, virtuous, and pray (see *Testimonies*, 2:562-564).

We are not sure what the girl did about the counsel received. We do not know whether she experienced true conversion. But an even more important question for present readers is whether we have some of the same problems, and whether we will profit from the encouragement given.

What are we to learn from the words of Christ to the woman taken in adultery? What are we to learn from the message to Laodicea? What are we to learn from the letter to this girl? It is this. No matter how bad we are, there is hope. The greatness of the gospel message through Jesus Christ is that we can be restored and made righteous through Him. But the offer is not forced upon us. We must willingly accept.

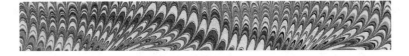

Introduction to Volume 3

1872-1875

No one could have imagined that Jesus would not have returned before this. Way back in 1859, someone sent the following question to the *Review*: "Is the Third Angel's Message . . . to be given except in the United States?"

Uriah Smith, the twenty-six-year-old editor, had replied: "We have no information that the Third Message is at present being proclaimed in any country besides our own. . . . this might not perhaps be necessary . . . since our own land is composed of people from almost every nation"—*Review*, February 3, 1859.

But the Lord had other plans. If they had looked for it, they would have seen a world work in Ellen White's 1848 vision that helped to launch the publishing work that was described as "streams of light that went clear round the world."

In one sense, that had been fulfilled, in the preparation of literature in several languages. But now it was time to send *people*. And in a dramatic way, the Lord even told us some of the places where we would go.

This volume contains personal counsel, like the one preceding it. One such message was sent to a scholar, who was in danger of becoming sidetracked into too much detail in defending the faith. When this counsel was first published, the name was included. In this volume, Ellen White adapted it as more general counsel.

But let's get on with a look at this and other messages that are still appropriate today.

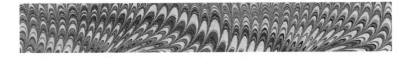

Letter to a Scholar

3T 32-39

Frequently, Ellen White adapted counsel written in a personal letter to be used for the general reader. The letter from which this chapter was taken was written, in 1872 (Letter 31, 1872). (Quoted in *Manuscript Releases*, 13:341-347.) At the time she wrote it, the recipient was the pastor of the South Lancaster, Massachusetts, church, where Atlantic Union College is now located. The pastor's wife, Angeline, died of a stroke earlier that year at age forty-eight. He had two children, Charles and Mary. Two years later, he went to Europe as our first official missionary. Of course, it was J. N. Andrews.

John Andrews was born in Poland, Maine, July 22, 1829. Because of poor health, he attended school only until the age of eleven. At age thirteen he was converted, and in 1844, accepted belief in the soon coming of Christ. His uncle Charles, a U. S. Congressman, encouraged John to follow a political career. He certainly had the talents for it.

In early 1845, at age fifteen, he read a tract on the Sabbath, written by T. M. Preble, and began observing the seventh-day Sabbath with teenage friends and members of his family at Paris, Maine. His name first appeared in the *Present Truth* when he was twenty on a letter to the editor, James White, dated October 16, 1849.The next year he wrote his first doctrinal presentation for the *Review*, titled "Thoughts on the Sabbath." He and Uriah Smith married sisters, Angeline and Harriet Stevens.

The first issue of the *Review* was published by James White in November, 1850, at Paris, Maine, where Andrews lived. When our first Adventist-owned-and-operated press was set up in Rochester, New York, Andrews was one of a publishing committee of three. The other two were Joseph Bates and James White. Andrews was single, almost twenty-three. By the time of his ordination, at age twenty-four, thirty-five of his articles had been published in the *Review*, mostly on the subject of the Sabbath. During his lifetime he wrote 300 articles in the *Review*, on many subjects, plus several books.

Though his formal schooling had been limited, Andrews was an avid student, often carrying books with him. He read the Bible through at least twenty-seven times, memorizing large portions of it. It is claimed that he could reproduce the entire New Testament from memory. He also learned seven languages, including Greek, Hebrew, and Latin.

In 1858 Andrews helped to launch "systematic benevolence," the forerunner of our tithing system. In 1864, during the American Civil War, he went to Washington, D. C., to the Provost Marshall, and was successful in getting recognition for Seventh-day Adventists as noncombatants. From 1867 to 1869 he served as the third president of the General Conference, after John Byington, and James White. He also was editor of the *Review* for a time.

But back to the letter. It is clear that Andrews needed balance in his writing. Skilled as he was, he had a tendency to go deeper into a subject than most of his readers could follow. And while endeavoring, to make it as perfect as possible, he delayed the second edition of his *History of the Sabbath*.

With *Testimonies for the Church*, volume 3 in hand, compare its wording with Ellen White's original letter to Andrews. Note how she adapts it to a general audience. The original wording of the letter is in brackets. "Many [My brother, you] are not doing the greatest amount of good because they [you] exercise the intellect in one direction and neglect to give careful attention to those things for which they [you] think they [you] are not adapted" (32).

Ellen White speaks of "some faculties that are weak" that are lying "dormant, because the work that should call them into exercise, and consequently give them strength, is not pleasant [to you]." She then lists four "powers of the mind," that need to be cultivated—"perception," "judgment," "memory," and "reasoning powers." She states that not all of these are being used by Andrews (33).

In the next two paragraphs, Ellen White speaks of balance in the use of these four powers, saying that there are "monomaniacs all over the country." Her definition? Men who are "sane upon every subject but one."

In her letter to Andrews, she says: "Brother Andrews, you fail to turn your powers to the best account. Your strength to concentrate your mind upon one subject to the exclusion of all others, is well in a degree, but . . ." Then she develops this idea in a broader way.

See how she speaks to Andrews (in brackets) compared to what is in print:

"But there are very few minds that can follow them [you], unless they have given [give] the subject the same depth of thought [you have done]. There is danger of such men [your] plowing, and planting the seed of truth so deep the tender, precious blade will never find the surface. [Your labor will be appreciated only by a few]" (35).

It is truly an amazing letter to one of our best scholars. For the rest of the letter, you can fill in his name yourself. But let's try to see why she wrote like she did.

From the earliest days there were many opponents of our Sabbath teaching. At the time Andrews was writing his defense of the Sabbath, the chief opponents were first-day Adventists. Andrews delayed getting his Sabbath book into print because he was anxious to answer every objection in detail. The next few pages of

Ellen White's letter are important for dealing with opponents, even today.

She describes them. "They do not engage in the warfare honorably." They are "unreasonable," "inconsistent," and "cover up the truth." They "give publicity to . . . statements, however untrue, unjust and even ridiculous . . . against the truth which they hate." They "deal in slander and misrepresentations." They "manufacture quibbles." "Immoralities exist among them to a fearful extent" (36, 37). Ellen White then says that labor for them, even if successful in bringing them to accept truth, would be a "calamity." She states why: "They would have to unlearn everything and learn anew, or they would cause us great trouble" (37).

Well, how do you meet such opposition successfully? She tells us how: "We are not wise to take from their hands, and pass them [manufactured quibbles] out to thousands who would never have thought of them had we not published them to the world." She says that these men "want to be brought to notice and to have us publish for them." "They will die out more speedily to be left unnoticed." Their "errors and falsehoods" should be "treated with silent contempt."

Then, she makes a revealing comment: "They do not want to be let alone. Opposition is the element that they love. If it were not for this, they would have but little influence"(37).

Can we think of similar opponents today? They are all around us. What valuable counsel she has given—even for the present!

There is still another interesting fact. Ellen White was speaking specifically of two men. In the original letter she named them—Carver and Preble. Yes, the same T. M. Preble who wrote the tract on the Sabbath that led fifteen-year-old Andrews to accept it. Preble did not stay with the Sabbath but became a bitter enemy of those who continued to observe it. A strange turn in the story, indeed!

Speaking of Preble in particular, Ellen White said: "We should, as far as possible, go forward as though there were not such people in existence." Then she modifies this statement somewhat: "There are occasions when their glaring misrepresentations will have to be met. When this is the case, it should be done promptly and briefly, and we should then pass on to our work."

Ellen White then states another principle of action that is important: "It is not the best policy to be so very explicit and say all upon a point that can be said, when a few arguments will cover the ground . . . You may remove every prop today and close the mouths of objectors so that they can say nothing, and tomorrow they will go over the same ground again" (37). What shall we then do? Ellen White suggests a "better plan": "Keep a reserve of arguments" (38).

She speaks of the real power behind such opponents: "Satan will stir up opponents enough to keep their [defenders of the faith] pens constantly employed, while other branches of the work will be left to suffer." She encouraged Andrews—and us—to have "the spirit of those men who were engaged in building the walls of Jerusalem. We are doing a great work, and we cannot come down."

When Ellen White urges Andrews to get the Sabbath history out immediately, it sounds as if she is writing to us today: "Men and women who engage in the business of life have not time to meditate, or even to read the word of God enough to understand all its important truths. Long, labored arguments will interest but a few; for the people have to read as they run" (38).

She continues: "Plain, pointed arguments, standing out as mileposts, will do more toward convincing minds generally than will a large array of arguments which cover a great deal of ground, but which none but investigating minds will have interest to follow."

She concludes her letter to Andrews, and us, by saying: "Our success will be in reaching *common* minds" (39).

J. N. Andrews died too young, at age fifty-four, while he was serving in Europe. It is obvious that Ellen White had great respect for him. She wrote, in 1878, that Andrews "was the ablest man in our ranks"—Letter 2a, 1878.

Eminent scholar that he was, J. N. Andrews needed correction too. Through it all, however, he remained one of Ellen White's strongest supporters in her prophetic role. We also can profit from the counsel she gave to him.

Not a Time to Debate

3T 212-221

On December 10, 1871, Ellen White had a vision at Bordoville, Vermont. Several chapters in this volume come from that vision. They represent a wide variety of counsel—some personal and some for the church at large. Note the variety from this one vision: "The Cause in New York" (48-67); "Experience not Reliable" (67-79); "The Work at Battle Creek" (85-98); "The Health Reform" (161-165); "Missionary Work" (202-211); "Effect of Discussions"(212-221); "Dangers and Duties of Youth" (221-227); "Self-Caring Ministers" (227-243); and "Inordinate Love of Gain" (243-251).

When these testimonies first appeared in print, the Seventh-day Adventist Church was poised to begin a world work by sending J. N. Andrews to Europe. We were past our infant days and our ministers were becoming more confident in their preaching of our distinctive message. But with increased self-assurance, problems came, especially for young ministers.

Some of them began to relish debates, or "discussions," with ministers of other denominations. " We have the truth, and we know it," was the attitude of many. Some found a certain excitement in arguing our faith in public debates. Many of these young ministers developed debate tactics not in harmony with Christian courtesy and grace. In this vision, Ellen White was shown some of their dangers.

She said: "They leave God out," "discussion is coveted, and they prefer this kind of labor above any other" (212). They "do not study the Bible with humility," and discussions "do not increase spirituality." She said: "They have the theory of truth prepared to whip an opponent." They "snap their whip to irritate and provoke." The debates, she said, "tend to make ministers self-sufficient." She saw that debaters make poor pastors, because they often become "sarcastic, course, and rough." Ellen White went on to say that "feelings were stirred" by debate, but "consciences were not convicted." She spoke of some debating ministers depending on "debate or opposition as does the inebriate [drunk] upon his dram [liquor]" (213-217). In other chapters taken from this vision she repeats the comparison with the drunkard several times (see pages 185, 186, and 227).

In this testimony, Ellen White extols the example of Christ: "He was never elated with applause or dejected by censure or disappointment" (217).

The same principles are valid today in presenting the gospel to others. Two of these debating ministers are of special interest. One of them, Moses Hull (mentioned on page 212), had already left the church when Ellen White was given this vision, and the other, Dudley M. Canright, would leave later. Let's review their experiences.

Moses Hull became an Adventist in 1857. He was ordained as a minister the next year, at age twenty-two, and preached for only five years, from 1858 to 1863. He left the church only a few months after the formal organization of the General Conference, in 1863. During his last two years of preaching, Ellen White sent him several letters regarding his doubts, undue trust in himself, and debates with spiritualists.

Hull was an eloquent preacher, in great demand. He did some writing on spiritualism and the state of the dead and was a delegate to the Battle Creek meeting in 1860, when we chose the name "Seventh-day Adventist." Ellen White's visions in November 1862, and June 1863, had messages for Moses Hull. From the November vision she especially warned him: "Never should one man be sent forth to combat with a spiritualist"—*Testimonies*, 1:428.

In 1862, while working with J. N. Loughborough, Hull had several debates, one with a Methodist minister on the immortality of the soul, and others with spiritualists. All were successful, at least in the winning of the debates. "Afterward," Loughborough reports, "it seemed to 'turn his head,' and he thought he would be a match for spiritualists anywhere"—*Pacific Union Recorder*, June 6, 1912.

Soon after, Hull visited a spiritualist to plan a debate. He confided to Loughborough: "Let them bring on their devils. I am enough for the whole of them." When Hull went to debate, he went alone, and was defeated. Afterward, he said: "I am ready to go out and advocate spiritualism"—ibid.

After Hull's defeat by the spiritualist, Ellen White wrote: "He came back charmed with the man and was as much fascinated as ever a bird was fascinated by a rattlesnake . . . We could not help him"—Letter 11, 1862.

Soon after this, Hull joined the spiritualists, and gained some prominence among them. More can be read of Ellen White's counsel to Hull in *Testimonies*, 1:426-439; 442, 443; and ibid., 2:625.

Dudley M. Canright became a Seventh-day Adventist at age 19. He began preaching two years later, in 1861, and was ordained to the ministry in 1865 at age twenty-four. In 1868, he started debating, and developed some skill at it. He seemed to be the most enthusiastic when he could debate. But his ministry was a checkered experience. Four times, between 1870 and 1882, he became discouraged and either threatened to, or actually quit preaching. This is the record:

1. December 1870, after a debate with a Presbyterian minister, he wanted to leave the church.

2. Summer 1873, he left preaching for two years after Ellen

White gave him correction in Colorado. We'll look at this incident more closely in a moment.

3. October 1880, while attending a school of oratory in Chicago, he expressed a desire to leave what he called "this unpopular message."

4. Fall 1882, he left preaching for two years to farm.

Canright's ministry was marked by a desire to be great and important. He wrote several tracts and two books and numerous articles for the *Review*. He was president of the Ohio Conference from 1878 to 1880. During this same time, he was one of only three members of the General Conference committee. The other two were S. N. Haskell and James White.

He was perhaps most comfortable in public debate, and yet, periodically expressed doubts about his faith, even after successful debates. Each time, after coming back, he claimed to have renewed confidence, only to become discouraged again. Elder G. I. Butler, wrote of Canright: "We have never known a man in all our lives who could change his mind so suddenly and so radically as Elder Canright"—*Review* Extra, December, 1887.

Butler said more: "He never could bear reproof with patience, or feel composed when his way was crossed. . . . Elder Canright had little respect for any one's opinion unless it coincided with his own. . . .He always hated reproof, hence bore it like a fractious child. . . . When everything went pleasantly, he could usually see things with clearness. When he was 'abused,' as he always thought he was when things did not go to suit him, the evidences of our faith began immediately to grow dim. . . . He was good in a fight, and appeared at best advantage when in a hot debate"—ibid.

While staying with James and Ellen White in the hills of Colorado, in 1873, Canright, and his wife, Lucretia, received a strong rebuke from Ellen White. You can read it in total in *Testimonies*, 3:304-329.

She told him: "I saw that from a child you have been self-confident, headstrong, and self-willed, and have followed your own mind. . . . As you looked at the work of Brother and Sister White you thought that you could see where you could have done better than they. Feelings have been cherished in your heart against them. . . . As you have seen their work, and heard the reproofs given to those who were wrong, you have questioned how you would bear such plain testimony. You decided that you could not receive it, and began to brace yourself against the manner of their laboring, and thus opened a door in your heart for suspicion, doubt, and jealousy of them and their work"—ibid., 305, 306.

After this correction, Canright left the ministry between 1874 and 1876. Then, he returned, and wrote for the *Review*, April 19, 1877, "Plain Talks to Murmurers," in which he vowed never to leave again. His wife, Lucretia, died of tuberculosis on March 29, 1879, at age thirty-one.

The next year, while attending Hamil's School of Oratory in Chicago, he preached to a Protestant congregation of 3,000. It was a powerful sermon, and the audience praised him lavishly. Afterward, in a shared room with D. W. Reavis, he talked of leaving the church. "I believe," he said, "I could be a great man were it not for our unpopular message."

Reavis was shocked, but responded: "D.M., the message made you what you are, and the day you leave it, you will retrace your steps to where it found you." The two men talked most of the night, and Canright decided to stay by.

On October 15, 1880, Ellen White wrote to him: "You have wanted to be too much, and make a show and noise in the world and as the result your sun will surely set in obscurity"—*Selected Messages*, 2:163.

In the fall of 1882, he once again confessed doubt about the Adventist Church and its message and went to farming for two years. In 1884, he was back in the ministry. Writing in the *Review*, December 2, 1884, he stated: "I'll never do this backing up any more. . . . If I ever go back from this I am lost."

In 1886, Ellen White dreamed that she saw Canright as a passenger on a ship. He believed the ship was going to sink and wanted to get on another one. The captain said that if he left the ship, he would be lost. This counsel is found in *Testimonies*, 5:571, 572. The application is obvious.

As Canright came to the 1886 Michigan camp meeting, he confided to a friend: "If I'm not elected president, I'm not going to preach for this church any more." G. I. Butler was elected president, and in February, 1887, Canright asked for his name to be dropped from the church.

He joined the Baptist Church almost immediately and began preaching the next month, at Otsego, Michigan. He was pastor there for 18 months. For another two and a half years he was pastor in Grand Rapids, Michigan. He never held any major office for the Baptists. He travelled to a few places to preach against Adventists, but was never very successful.

In 1889, he published a book against Adventists in which he made a strangely insincere admission. He tells of the two years between 1882 and 1884, when he dropped out of the ministry to work on a farm. Then he writes of his confession and return to the church: "In the fall of 1884, Elder Butler, my old friend, and now at the head of the Advent work, made a great effort to get me reconciled and back at work again. He wrote me several times, to which I made no answer. Finally he telegraphed me, and paid my fare to a camp meeting. Here I met old friends and associations, tried to see things as favorable as possible, heard explanations, etc. etc., till at last I yielded again. I was sick of an undecided position. I thought I could do some good here anyway; all my friends were here; I believed most of the doctrine still, and I might go to ruin if I left them, etc. Now I resolved to swallow all my doubts, believe the whole thing anyway, and stay with them for better or worse. So I made a strong confession, *of which I was ashamed before it was cold"*—*Seventh-day Adventism Renounced*, 49 (emphasis supplied).

In this confession he had declared: " *I am fully satisfied* that my own salvation and my usefulness in saving others depends upon my being connected with this people and this work." He spoke of his reconversion as "the most remarkable change that I ever experienced in all my life."

After the meeting at which this confession was made, he asked for it to be published in the *Review*. He wrote also of his understanding of the working of the Holy Spirit: "I believe it was directly from heaven—the work of the Spirit of God"—*Review*, October 7, 1884.

A strange admission indeed!

Later, Canright worked on another book. This one was against Ellen White. While working on it, he attended her funeral at Battle Creek, on July 24, 1915. At the funeral he was heard to say, as he wept at the casket: "There is a noble Christian woman gone." Then he went back to completing his book against her!

After his defection from the Seventh-day Adventist Church, Canright boasted of various exaggerated achievements as an Adventist. For example, he wrote of being an instructor in biblical exegesis at Battle Creek College. His total teaching time was eight weeks. He spoke of being a leading minister that the Adventist Church could hardly afford to lose. In early years, he had been prominent, but for the last sixteen years, when in and out of the ministry, he had been largely ineffective.

In 1916, he had a accident that left him an invalid. He finished his book against Ellen White in 1918. In 1919 he died in near poverty, depending largely on Doctor Kellogg at the Battle Creek Sanitarium for most of his meals. His book was printed that year. Ellen White's prediction that his "sun would set in obscurity" proved to be correct.

Even Canright's grave marker is a reflection of the contradictions in his life. It reads: "Elder D. M. Canright, September 22, 1840-May 12, 1919. An Author of World Renown." The title "Elder" is one from the Adventist Church. The books that made him supposedly of "world renown" were written against the same Adventist Church.

The rest of Ellen White's published counsel to Canright can be found in *Testimonies*, 3:304-329; *Selected Messages*, 2:162-170; *Testimonies*, 5:516-520; 571-573; and 621-628.

Both Moses Hull and Dudley Canright illustrate the dangers of debate. Hull preached between the ages of twenty-two and twenty-seven, while Canright preached for the Adventists between the ages of twenty-one and forty-six. They were contemporaries in preaching for two years, between 1861 and 1863.

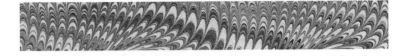

An Astounding Vision

3T 468-471

Especially in her earlier prophetic ministry, any single one of Ellen White's visions might contain messages of great variety. This variety is evident in a vision received on January 3, 1875. *Testimonies for the Church*, volume three, contains about one hundred and forty pages, based on the vision. But there is still more. Most of the first half of volume four also is based on this vision. Just in these two volumes, as many as three hundred pages can be traced to the same vision. And that isn't all. Several letters of counsel, not in print, refer to that vision on the afternoon of January 3, 1875.

We might think that such a vision would have lasted for several hours so that the large variety of content could be given. But the amazing fact is that it all took place in only ten minutes! How could such detail be given in so short a time? Both Ellen White and her son W. C. White, a witness to this vision, have given us help in answering the question. Ellen White once wrote: "The question is asked, How does Sister White know in regard to the matters of which she speaks so decidedly, as if she had authority to say these things? I speak thus because *they flash upon my mind* when in perplexity like lightning out of a dark cloud in the fury of a storm."

She continues: "Some scenes presented before me years ago have not been retained in my memory, but when the instruction then given is needed, sometimes even when I am standing before the people, the remembrance comes sharp and clear, *like a flash of lightning*, bringing to mind distinctly that particular instruction" —*Selected Messages*, 3:43 (emphasis supplied).

Her son W. C. White uses a similar phrase in speaking of her writing the controversy story: "The things which she has written out, are descriptions of flashlight pictures and other representations given her regarding the actions of men, and the influence of these actions upon the work of God for the salvation of men, with views of past, present, and future history in its relation to this work"—ibid., footnote.

Writing about how she presented her visions, she said: "I am just as dependent upon the Spirit of the Lord in relating or writing a vision, as in having the vision. It is impossible for me to call up things which have been shown me unless the Lord brings them before me at the time that He is pleased to have me relate or write them"—*Spiritual Gifts*, 2:293.

So, the Spirit of the Lord helped her both when the vision was given, and when she presented the content, whether in speaking or writing. It could be concluded that in both of these circumstances, the Lord is able to present the subject in more detail.

The statement at the beginning of this testimony, begins: "I was shown many things relative to the great and important interests at Battle Creek in the work of the Publishing Association" —*Testimonies*, 3:468.

We could look in some depth at any one of the subjects of this vision. But the circumstances under which it was given suggest what might be considered one of the most important subjects in its wide-ranging content—the development of publishing around the world.

At the time of this vision, Seventh-day Adventists had one

publishing house in all the world. We had one sanitarium. Both were in Battle Creek. Three and one-half months earlier we had sent our first missionary—J. N. Andrews. And we had just built our first college—again in Battle Creek.

On April 1, 1874, Ellen White had been shown that the Adventist message was to be given in other countries, and established there. (See *Life Sketches*, 208-210.) No doubt there were some church members who questioned whether we should build a college when the second advent seemed so near. When Andrews was sent as our first foreign missionary to Europe on September 15, 1874, some probably questioned this decision too.

But, beginning in 1871, at the urging of Ellen White, a search for property for a college had begun. In harmony with her counsel, they were searching for a farm, with a large acreage, away from the city. Many properties were examined. Her son W. C. White recalls that a farm was located on Goagac Lake for $1,500, but as the leaders hesitated, the farm was sold to others. Later, another farm became available for $20,000. Again, because of indecision, the farm was sold (W. C. White statement at the Advanced Bible School, July, 1934, Document file 105b).

In the winter of 1873, while James and Ellen White were in California, about thirteen acres, owned by the Huzzey family, became available. This property, right across from the sanitarium, in the center of Battle Creek, was bought. Half of it was promptly resold for homes for teachers. It was not the kind of location she had encouraged. James White wrote in the *Review* that Ellen wept bitterly when she learned that the college was not planning for the type of location she had suggested.

Work was begun in the spring of 1874 on the main college building. The dedication of the college was planned for late 1874, but cold weather and snow caused some postponement. Ellen White was asked to speak at the dedication. It is significant that she agreed to do so, even though the college had not been built where she had urged. It demonstrates that she had not given up on the project, even though everything was not ideal.

Several days before the planned dedication, a flu epidemic swept through Battle Creek, and many became sick. For most, the flu lasted only three or four days. Ellen White became sick, but, after a few days, she seemed to be worse rather than better.

Finally, the day before the planned dedication—January 3, 1875—James decided to ask Uriah Smith and J. H. Waggoner to accompany him to their home for prayer. Ellen White was brought down to the big front room of their house on the corner of Washington and Champion Streets. Willie, her twenty-year-old son, and his older brother, twenty-five-year-old Edson, as well as two or three others joined the group.

Both Waggoner and Smith prayed. Then, James prayed. Finally, Ellen White began to pray, first in a hoarse whisper. After only two or three sentences, her voice was heard, loud and clear: "Glory to God! Glory to God!" Her son, Willie says: "We looked up, and saw that she was in vision."

Her eyes were open and looking up, her lips tightly closed, and her arms folded across her chest. She threw off her blanket and stood to her feet, walking back and forth across the room. At first, she had a distressed look on her face. Finally, she spoke: "Dark, dark, so dark." Then she began to smile, and spoke again: "Light. A little light. More light. Much light!" At the conclusion of the ten-minute vision, she took three long breaths, and then began breathing naturally.

James tried to find out what she had seen. "Do you want to tell us about it?" he asked. "Not now," was her reply. She was helped back to her room, and the men returned to the office.

About suppertime, James returned to the house, and went to her room. He found her writing at her desk. She had been healed. When he asked if she would like to attend the evening meeting at the church, she agreed to go. They walked through newly fallen snow to the meeting. When they arrived, she was asked to tell about the vision of the day. She replied that she would share it the next day at the college dedication.

The next day, Uriah Smith gave a fifteen-minute welcoming address. James White spoke briefly. Then Ellen White spoke. The meeting house that held about three hundred and fifty was full. She spoke of the work of the church, and that it should be broader than what some had understood. Men were to be educated for the ministry and sent to all parts of the world. The printing work was to be expanded. Then she spoke of seeing printing presses in her vision operating in many countries. James interrupted her, and asked if she could recall any of the countries. She hesitated a moment, and then replied that she remembered the angel speaking of Australia.

There was no Adventist work in Australia to that point. Elder S. N. Haskell was at the college dedication services, and determined that he would begin the work in that country. Ten years later, in 1885, together with Elder J. O. Corliss, Haskell sailed through the Golden Gate in San Francisco to Australia.

Ellen White, herself, would go to Europe, also in 1885. We had erected a new headquarters in Basel, Switzerland. As she came to the building, she said to those who were with her: "Why, I have seen this building before." When they reached the pressroom, the press was running, and she said: "I have seen this press before." When two young men entered the room, and were introduced to her, she inquired: "Where is the other one?"

Elder B. L. Whitney, superintendent of the European Mission, who was accompanying her, asked: "What other one?" "There is an older man here, and I have a message for him," she said. The next day when she met the other man, she gave him a message from her vision of *ten years before*.

A few months later, when she visited our publishing house in Oslo, Norway, she recognized the presses there too. She had counsel for their needs as well.

When she went to Australia, six years later, and visited the Echo Publishing House in Melbourne, she recognized the presses there from her vision, she had counsel for them too—*Life Sketches*, 282, 283.

Ellen White didn't live long enough to see all of the publishing houses that are in operation today around the world. Wouldn't it be interesting to discover how many of them she would recognize from this vision?

Perhaps one of the most important lessons to be learned from this experience is that Ellen White didn't give up on the church leaders when they failed to build our college on a large piece of property. It is a reminder that God doesn't give up on us when we don't follow His way for us perfectly from the start.

But there are other lessons as well. When this vision was given, it was time to broaden our horizons to a world work. Given at the time of the opening of our first college, it afforded an opportunity to encourage the students of that college to train for world ministry, which many did. This college, and many others that have followed, continue to train both men and women for service.

There is still another lesson for then and now. As Ellen White traveled to other parts of the world, she had opportunity, first, to see the fulfillment of the vision, and second, to impress on the minds of those who were there, that God anticipated their needs even before they occurred, and was ready to supply them when the time came. He is surely ready and able to do the same for us today.

Introduction to Volume 4

1875-1881

Because the Bible narrative is often condensed, we do not usually get well acquainted with prophets. Ellen White chose, however, to tell her own personal story. This volume was written during the last seven years of her husband's life, when he had suffered strokes that affected his personality and disposition. This was the great camp meeting era. One time the Whites decided to travel separately, so they could get to more places. But James didn't want to do it again, because, he said, "They wanted to hear you, Ellen." How would you like to be a prophet's husband?

It was also an especially tender time, when Ellen White sometimes laid aside her other work, to care for her ailing husband. When she was once asked how she felt about James, she replied: "No better man ever trod shoe leather." James referred to her as "my crown of rejoicing." In 1881 she had to lay him in the grave, and then go on alone. It would be thirty-four years more before she could lay down her work.

The other story we share begins in the 1860s, when Ellen was shown a reform dress in vision. It was the age of hoop skirts, long dresses dragging on the street, and tiny "wasp waists" created by tight corsets that hardly allowed women to breathe. How do you try to tell a whole generation of women how to dress when the fashion world disagrees? Not easy. Some reform was accomplished, but when it threatened to turn us from more important issues, Ellen White no longer advocated the "reform dress."

Still, her counsel for modesty, good taste, and simplicity, has significance for us today, both male and female. The principles that she emphasized continue to be appropriate.

"Dear Diary"

4T 271-305

The "good old days" a hundred years ago were times of inconvenience, slowness of travel, and, for many, poor health. Several Adventist pioneers suffered from health problems of one kind or another. James and Ellen White were no exception. All her life, Ellen White endured a variety of illnesses. Her serious accident in early childhood, when struck by a stone, left her weak and unable to continue school after about the age of nine. At various periods of her life, she experienced heart and lung problems, voice difficulties and other ailments. No doubt, some of her sickness originated from her early accident, but when she began her work, the Lord promised to bring affliction to her if she were ever tempted to be proud. Some might be traced to this promise. (See *Testimonies for the Church*, 1:65.)

James White had several strokes and went through a physical breakdown in his forties. He also had periodic illness, sometimes brought on by overwork and the stress of leading a fledgling church. And yet, what they accomplished in the face of these difficulties is truly remarkable. In this chapter of the *Testimonies*, she opens up her diary for a very busy eighteen-month period of time.

The diary begins on May 11, 1877, with the Whites traveling by train from Oakland, California, to Battle Creek, Michigan. For several months before the trip, she had heart pains and breathing problems. James also was in poor health. He was now fifty-five, and she was forty-nine years of age. James was also president of the General Conference. They were responding to a telegram that had asked him to carry on church business.

When they arrived in Battle Creek, they stayed with friends because their house had been rented to another family. Upon arrival, James plunged into a busy program that included preaching, writing for the *Review*, and attending board meetings at the *Review* office, the college, and the sanitarium, often going late into the night. His reserve of strength was fast running out.

Finally, for health reasons, they decided that they must get away for some rest. They would go to the mountains of Colorado. But a voice said to her: "I have work for you to do in Battle Creek." She turned, expecting to see a person, but no one was there. Then she knew that the Lord was speaking to her. She told her husband what had happened. They were due to leave in three days. But after weeping and praying together, she said: "All our plans were changed."

What did the Lord have for her to do in Battle Creek? The answer was not long in coming. On May 30, patients and staff of the sanitarium went to Goguac Lake, two miles away, for a recreational outing. The sanitarium at that time was really a health training and rehabilitation center, not an acute care hospital. She was asked to speak. She used the occasion to draw lessons from the ministry of Jesus, as He healed the sick and spoke to them by the Sea of Galilee. One of the patients, a judge from Wisconsin, was so impressed that he requested that the talk be printed for the benefit of others. This was done.

The third school year at Battle Creek College was about to close. She held a week of evening meetings for the students. She says: "I tried to impress upon them that a life of purity and prayer would not be a hindrance to them in obtaining a thorough knowledge of the sciences, but that it would remove many hindrances to their progress in knowledge"—*Testimonies*, 4:273.

At the end of the week, fourteen students were baptized, with several others choosing to be baptized at their home churches later. "But," she says, "My work was not yet done at Battle Creek" (274).

And so it turned out to be. On June 28, Barnum's menagerie came to town. The Battle Creek Reform Club (600 members) and the Women's Christian Temperance Union (260 members) arranged a temperance meeting to reach the large crowd anticipated for the circus.

The WCTU set up a restaurant in a tent provided by the Michigan Conference. Fifteen to twenty tables of food were arranged in the tent. A thirty-foot table was set up in the center by the Battle Creek Sanitarium. It was loaded with fruits, grains, and vegetables and proved to be the main attraction. Another twenty-foot table was added, and they were both quickly crowded.

Mayor Austin, chairman of the arrangement committee, asked Ellen White to speak in the tent on the evening of July 1. She spoke on Christian temperance for ninety minutes to a crowd of 5,000. It continued to be clear why the Lord had told her: "I have work for you to do in Battle Creek" (275).

Then a call came for the Whites to go to the Indiana camp meeting, but James was too ill to attend. So Ellen White traveled with her daughter-in-law, Mary—Willie's wife—to the camp meeting. She spoke several times. On Monday morning, August 13, she had a severe cold, but she pled with the Lord to help her once again. She spoke, and fifty came forward for prayer. Fifteen were baptized afterward. These camp meetings were more like evangelistic meetings in those early years, sometimes with large numbers of non-Adventists in attendance.

Calls came to attend camp meetings in Ohio and the East, but she decided to return to Battle Creek for treatment at the sanitarium. All the time she was at the Indiana camp meeting, James was busy at Battle Creek, though he was not well. After her return, he preached on Sabbath, August 18, and then, for four hours in the afternoon, he listened to the reading of the manuscript for her next book, *Spirit of Prophecy*, volume 3, being prepared for publication.

On Sunday, James started work again at 5 a.m., and continued till midnight. Early Monday morning, he experienced dizziness, and seemed about to suffer another stroke, but he was spared. The experience left him physically and mentally exhausted. Friends pled with the Whites to stay in Battle Creek to recuperate their strength.

At this time, a letter came from S. N. Haskell, inviting them to come to Groveland, Massachusetts. All preparations had been made for a large camp meeting. Haskell had experience in such planning. A year earlier, he had organized a similar meeting at Groveland. The story of that earlier meeting is an interesting one.

Ellen White had spoken there, to a crowd estimated at 20,000 in a great open air "pavilion"—a grove of oak and pine trees. It was the largest crowd in her ministry. Train tracks of the Boston and Maine railroad ran along one side of the grove. It also was located near a river, so that ferry boats could bring people to the meetings.

As the time approached, Elder Haskell had made out a list of special favors that he hoped to get from the railroad company. With another minister, he went to see Mr. Ferber, the railroad president.

The list filled two sheets of legal-sized paper. It asked that two large carloads of freight be transferred free of charge from the storage room at South Lancaster, Massachusetts, about forty miles away. He wanted everything taken back after the meetings were over. He also requested free passes for conference and committee men, and half fare permits for campers coming from a distance. They would need trains run on Sunday, with extra trains run during the week. Haskell also asked for a platform to be built beside the track, and water piped to the grounds.

Mr. Ferber looked over the list and frowned a bit, and then sent the men to the manager's office. When he read over the list, he exclaimed: "Gentlemen, why don't you ask for the world?"

Haskell replied: "Oh, we thought we would be a little modest." In the end, the men got everything they asked for, except that the platform was not quite as long as they had requested.

When the meetings started, river steamers ran twice daily from Haverhill, and every hour on Sunday—a day set aside for evangelistic meetings. Hundreds of private carriages also came. Eighteen trains ran each day, all stopping at the campground. The 2:30 train on Sunday afternoon had fifteen cars, all packed. The platform and steps were so full that the conductor had to climb on the roof of the train in order to signal the engineer. (See *S. N. Haskell, Man of Action*, 33, 34.)

There was one difficulty, however, that had not been anticipated—food for the great multitude. After the morning trains began arriving on Sunday, it was clear that there would not be enough food. Large quantities of food were ordered from Haverhill. But though many took the trains home for dinner, those who remained, according to a reporter, "swept down on the eatables like an army of grasshoppers on a Kansas corn-field, and made quite as clean work. . . . Elder Haskell, though famous for happy expedients, was unable to feed the multitudes with a few loaves and fishes"—*The Signs of the Times*, September 14, 1876.

But now, it is a year later. Another camp meeting is planned at the same location in Groveland. James White is feeble. Ellen is weary, sick, and somewhat discouraged. A carriage waits to take them to the train depot in Battle Creek. What should they do? They pray earnestly about it and decide to go. After they board the train, assurance comes that God is leading. It is Wednesday. They arrive in Boston on Friday evening.

Sabbath morning, they take the train to Groveland in a "pouring" rain. On Sunday, August 26, Ellen White writes that the boats and trains "poured" people onto the grounds. From a pouring of rain, it becomes a pouring of people.

A tent, 80 by 120 feet, has been erected. As she walks onto the platform on Sunday afternoon, the tent is full and thousands crowd around the outside to hear her speak. Her lungs and throat are giving her great pain, but as she steps forward, and in answer to a silent prayer, she receives the strength to preach. "While speaking," she afterward said, "my weariness and pain were forgotten as I realized that I was speaking to a people that did not regard my words as idle tales" (279). She spoke for over an hour to the huge crowd.

On Monday morning, she engaged in personal work for the 200 who had come forward in response to her call for prayer. They ranged in age from "ten to gray-headed men and women." In the afternoon, thirty-eight were baptized. Many more were baptized later in their hometowns.

Monday evening, she traveled by train with D. M. Canright to his evangelistic meetings at Danvers, Massachusetts. But upon leaving Groveland for Danvers, she knew that she was very sick. What could she do? Upon arrival, she prayed for strength, and went to the front of the meeting place as the last song was being sung. She tells what happened next: "The Spirit of the Lord rested upon me as I attempted to speak. Like a shock of electricity I felt it upon my heart, and all pain was instantly removed" (281). She spoke to a full tent of people, with two hundred more crowded outside, for an hour and ten minutes.

Then it was off to camp meetings in Morrisville, Vermont; Carthage, New York; and Lansing, Michigan. In Lansing, she spoke to crowds from six thousand to ten thousand. This was followed by the sixteenth General Conference Session, also at Lansing. She spoke for it as well.

She and her husband returned to Battle Creek where she spoke again on October 6. Then she was off to Oakland, California in middle October. She visited churches in Petaluma, Santa Rosa, Healdsburg, Saint Helena, and Vacaville during the remainder of the year. *Spirit of Prophecy*, volume 2, was published late in the year. In December, she moved to Healdsburg.

Ellen White worked with her husband, James, in the early months of 1878 in California. His health continued to be a great burden to both of them. On May 31, he left for Battle Creek to do church business, and she made plans to go to Oregon.

In 1874, four years earlier, she had been given an impressive dream. She saw church leaders in council making plans for the future. A young man she had often seen in vision, came into the council. He spoke of the cities, large and small, and the need to carry the gospel to the world. He warned that they were making too limited plans. He said: "Your light must not be put under a bushel or under a bed, but on a candlestick, that it may give light to all that are in the house. Your house is the world."

Then he said something that would seem unusual to us today: "The message will go in power to all parts of the world, to Oregon, to Europe, to Australia, to the islands of the sea, to all nations, tongues, and peoples"—*Life Sketches*, 209.

What was that again? Oregon, a mission field? It surely was at that time—in every sense of the word. Now, four years later, Ellen White was instructed to become a "missionary" to Oregon. She sailed out of San Francisco harbor on June 10 on the *S.S. Oregon*. She describes passing through the Golden Gate, "As we passed through the Golden Gate into the broad ocean, it was very rough. The wind was against us, and the steamer pitched fearfully, while the ocean was lashed into fury by the wind. I watched the clouded sky, the rushing waves leaping mountain high, and the spray reflecting the colors of the rainbow. The sight was fearfully grand!" (287). Ellen White loved to travel.

Her "missionary trip" to Oregon was to have great variety. She had meetings with the small number of Adventists there, spoke twice in a Methodist church, and several times at the first Oregon camp meeting. This meeting was held near Salem with 2,000 people in attendance, most of whom were not Adventists. Later, a meeting was arranged in the public square in Salem, where 250 people listened to her. She was also invited to visit the state prison near Salem, where she spoke to 150 prisoners.

Upon returning to California in mid-July, she made immediate plans to go east. Traveling with her daughter-in-law, Emma—wife of her son, Edson—along the way she had speaking appointments in Sacramento, California; Reno, Nevada; and Boulder City, Colorado, where she briefly rejoined her husband, James. Then it was on to Battle Creek to speak again. Next, there were camp meetings in Ballard Vale, Massachusetts; and Waterville, Maine, with a brief stop in her hometown of Portland, Maine. Then she took a speaking appointment at Rome, New York, and returned to Battle Creek on September 18. There, she spoke several times at the national camp meeting which was held October 2-14. She spoke at other meetings there, as well.

She left Battle Creek again, on October 23. She preached to 150 at a camp meeting in Richland, Kansas, and to 200 at a camp meeting at Sherman, Kansas. The eighteen-month chronicle ends at Plano, Texas, November 19, 1878, with still another camp meeting attended by 200 persons. We must again be reminded that these camp meetings were not gatherings of Adventists for revival, but were evangelistic in nature, with large numbers of nonchurch members in attendance.

There is a most interesting fact we must not overlook. Our world membership, which included 150 in the Swiss Mission, under J. N. Andrews's direction, was 10,044 in 1876. Two years later, at the end of 1878, the world membership was 13,077. This was an increase of a few over three thousand. As a direct result of Ellen White's evangelism, *in this same time period*, and by her count, at least three hundred and thirty-eight were baptized in response to her appeals. That's eleven percent of the total increase for the world!

Ellen White was an evangelist, bringing people to Christ. Whether she was encouraging a girl to attend Battle Creek College, or a crowd of thousands, she carried the soul-winning burden. All of this she accomplished while she was fragile, and often very ill. She was often tested by the Lord. She never failed Him, and He never failed her. And so ends her eighteen-month diary.

More Than a Dress

4T 628-649

From its beginning in the Garden of Eden, dress has been a problem. As sinners, Adam and Eve tried to clothe themselves because they were naked and ashamed. Even then, they did not make the right choice, and God had to provide a better covering for them.

In the Bible, counsel regarding dress is given almost exclusively to women. The same is true in the writings of Ellen White. And yet, there are right principles for both men and women to accept.

When the Seventh-day Adventist Church was born, in the 1850s and 1860s, women's dress fashions were receiving major attention in the United States. The styles of the time called for multilayered, heavy, cumbersome dresses, suspended at the waist, with breath-restricting corsets underneath. Hoops further limited movement, and were immodest, especially for getting in and out of carriages. Dresses dragged in the dust, mud, or snow, depending on the season. They were expensive, unhealthful, and inconvenient.

The times called for a reform in women's dress. Some of the prominent names in the dress reform movement included Mrs. Elizabeth Miller (daughter of a U. S. Congressman), Elizabeth Cady

Stanton, and Amelia Bloomer. Their efforts to bring change date back as early as 1851. Doctor Harriet Austin, an adopted daughter of Doctor James C. Jackson, and associated with him at a Health Institute in Dansville, New York, was another woman who joined in advocating style changes.

In 1862, a women's dress reform advocate, spoke with humor: "Women's clothing is arranged with such an eye to inconvenience and burdensomeness, that if they go out at all it is under great disadvantage. If they should cross the threshold, they may dampen their feet and soil their skirts on the steps, and have their unprotected limbs chilled by the wind. If they wish to walk, they must wait till the dew is off the grass, and a sultry summer sun detracts from the benefit of it. If they work in the garden, more strength is expended on account of the dress than with the plants; for it is not only so arranged that they cannot make a motion easily, but it must be gathered up in their arms while they work with their hands. If they go to the market, they must carry skirts as well as a basket; for dew, dust, mud, or snow has to be cleared. If they ride, they must be lifted in and out of their carriage, while they take care of their skirts, and even then they are often caught, and have to be extricated from them. . . .

"They must zigzag their way around every bush and log, in spending all their care on muslin instead of enjoying nature; and if they come to a fence, the field beyond is forbidden ground to them, though it be all abloom with choicest flowers"—Ellen Beard Harmon Lecture. (See *The Story of Our Health Message*, 112,113.)

There were times when Ellen White looked at the question of dress with much the same humor. In 1864, she wrote: "Sisters when about their work should not put on clothing which would make them look like images to frighten the crows from the corn"—*Testimonies*, 1:464.

Writing the next year, she said: "There is a class . . . who think it a virtue to be dirty, and dress without order and taste; and their clothing often looks as though it flew and lit upon their persons"—*Selected Messages*, 2:474.

Ellen White began speaking about dress reform as early as 1856. This counsel focused on display and pride in dress. (See *Testimonies*, 1:131-136.). After her major health reform vision of June 6, 1863, the emphasis shifted more to health. In 1864, she placed a brief chapter in *Testimony* number 10 on extremes in dress. (See ibid., 424-426). That same year, when she reprinted the larger portion of her first ten testimony pamphlets as a part of *Spiritual Gifts*, volume 4, she included a chapter titled "Health," in which she wrote in some detail of what she had seen on the subject of dress. (See *Spiritual Gifts*, 4:120-151.)

In 1864, James and Ellen White decided to visit a Health Institute at Dansville, New York, operated by Dr. J. C. Jackson. They spent three weeks there, observing his methods and practices. It was here that they were first exposed to Doctor Harriet Austin's reform dress known as the "American costume." This dress consisted of pants, a vest, and a dress that extended to half way between the hips and knees. It had the appearance of a man's suit, and Ellen White objected to it as "too mannish." She said: "I saw that God's order had been reversed, and His special directions disregarded, by those who adopt the American costume. I was referred to Deuteronomy 22:5: 'The woman shall not wear that which pertaineth unto a man, neither shall a man put on a woman's garment: for all that do so are abomination unto the Lord thy God ' "—*Testimonies*, 1:421.

The next year, 1865, the Whites produced a series of six pamphlets, titled "How to Live." They contained excerpts from leading health writers of the day. In each one, Ellen White provided one article with the general title: "Disease and Its Causes." Part of the fifth article and all of the sixth were dedicated to dress. The sixth article began:

"My sisters, there is need of a dress reform among us. There are many errors in the present style of female dress"—*Selected Messages*, 2:473.

Later that same year James White suffered a stroke and the Whites spent three months at Dansville, with him now as a patient. As Ellen

White had more time to observe the "American costume," advocated by Doctor Austin, her opposition strengthened, and she decided to offer a reform dress more in keeping with what she had seen in vision.

Mrs. White even made a pattern for this dress. What she provided was more feminine in appearance, with the dress extending to about eight-to-ten inches from the floor. It was suspended from the shoulders, with no hoops, or the restrictions of a corset, that provided the slender "wasp waist" look of the day. Under the skirt were pants that extended to the top of the shoe. This provided protection for the lower legs. For about ten years she promoted this dress, or some variation of it.

In 1867, Ellen White wrote two more articles on dress (see *Testimonies*, 1:456-466, and 521-525). That same year, she spoke about the reform dress in a *Review* article, in question and answer form. In vision she had seen three groups of women, each wearing a different style of dress. She said: "The first were of fashionable length, burdening the limbs, impeding the step, and sweeping the street and gathering its filth. . . . This class, who were slaves to fashion, appeared feeble and languid"—*Review*, October 8, 1867.

"The dress of the second class which passed before me," she said, "was in many respects as it should be. The limbs were well clad. They were free from the burdens which the tyrant, Fashion, had imposed upon the first class; but had gone to that extreme in the short dress as to disgust and prejudice good people, and destroy in a great measure their own influence. This is the style and influence of the 'American costume' taught and worn by many at 'Our Home' in Dansville, New York. It does not reach to the knee. I need not say that this style of dress was shown me to be too short.

"A third class passed before me," she continued, "with cheerful countenance, and free, elastic step. Their dress was the length I have described as proper, modest, and healthful. It cleared the filth of the street and sidewalk a few inches under all circumstances, such as ascending and descending steps"—ibid.

But now, we turn to the counsel found in this chapter, published fourteen years later, in 1881. It continues to characterize the best dress as "simple, neat, modest, becoming, healthful, and appropriate."

But there is, to some readers, a surprising feature of this article
she was no longer advocating the "reform dress" of earlier years. Several things had taken place in the intervening years. More healthful
dress styles had been accepted. Many of the extremes had all but disappeared. But also, dress reform had only been partially accepted by
Adventist women. In this article she reminded them: "Dress reform
comprised *more than* shortening the dress and clothing the limbs" (635).

The Lord had given instructions through Ellen White that
women were to wear *shorter* dresses! The reform dress, in fact,
was to average nine inches *shorter* than the styles of the day! This
reminds us that in reading, we need to look beyond the words to
the principles involved. Otherwise we are in danger of imposing
on the counsel something that was not intended.

But why had the reform dress been laid aside? Again, Ellen
White provides some answers in this chapter. Here are some of the
reasons.

1. There was controversy because some accepted it and some
did not.

2. Many only shortened dresses and clothed their limbs.

3. Some sought to control the conscience of others.

4. Extremists had made dress their religion.

5. Some became proud of being different.

6. The reform dress was a grave yoke to others.

7. Some lacked order and neatness, with ill-proportioned, out
of taste, grotesque dresses.

8. Diversity was too extreme.

9. The murmuring and complaining were destroying godliness.

Though dress has often been largely a woman's issue, the "beholder" is to be considered too. Ellen White says: "Showy, ex-
travagant dress too often encourages lust in the heart of the wearer,
and awakens passions in the heart of the beholder" (645).

And so, the reform dress is dead. It has been dead for more
than one hundred years. Other styles can be worn in good taste
today. Even when writing during the heat of the dress reform de-

bate, Ellen White suggested that we should "not take pains to make ourselves gazing stocks," but "if the world introduces a modest, convenient, and healthful mode of dress, which is in accordance with the Bible, it will not change our relation to God or to the world to adopt such a style of dress"—*Review*, October 8, 1867.

In this chapter we are studying, Ellen White says: "Obedience to fashion is pervading our Seventh-day Adventist Church and is doing more than any other power to separate our people from God" (647). We should soberly consider whether that problem still exists today, more than one hundred years later. Certainly the whole dress controversy has its lessons yet. Here are some:

1. Motives. In the area of dress, as in all others, we must examine our motives. Why do we dress in a certain way? Is it to glorify God, or draw attention to ourselves?

2. Principles. Again, to understand both what the Bible says, and the modern prophetic messenger, we must look beyond the words to the principles. Times *do* change, and styles and circumstances are not always constant. What may be appropriate or modest, or in good taste for one time may not always apply to another.

3. Identification. Who are we? What message do we want to give to others? Some styles in all ages identify us with certain things. In the mid-1800s, for example, wearing the "American costume" identified women with spiritualists, or with the women's rights movement. At all times, it is right to wear what identifies us as Christians.

4. Health. Do we dress for the well-being of our bodies, both externally and internally? Certain practices at any period of history disregard health for the sake of being "acceptable" to our peers.

5. Modesty. The dictionary definition of modesty does not talk about how much of the body is exposed. It talks, instead, about clothing being appropriate and in good taste. We must always remember that what we wear not only affects ourselves, but the "eye of the beholder."

Surely, in dress, as in all other areas, the right thing to do is more important than any other consideration. God wants us to be happy. He would not require something of us that was not for our good.

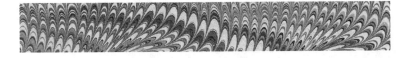

Introduction to Volume 5

1882-1889

When Adventists gathered at Minneapolis, Minnesota, for the General Conference of 1888, there were all the elements present for a crisis. A. T. Jones and E. J. Waggoner, young ministers from California, joined in a frontal assault on the "old guard" of the church, both regarding prophecy and how to be saved.

Uriah Smith, a leader of the "old guard," took exception to these two young men who preached "righteousness by faith." To this point, Adventists had been the most ardent defenders of the law of God, with many taking a legalistic stance.

Ellen White found herself in the middle of the controversy, because she came down on the side of the young men, against her old friend, Uriah Smith, and others. Smith began to question her ministry, and he voiced his doubts to others. That's part of the reason she published a lengthy review of her prophetic ministry. In a sense, the authenticity of her testimonies was on the line.

The church in the northwest United States was also developing. A large section of this volume contains counsel relating to it. This was the time of the final apostasy of D. M. Canright. Some counsel to him is found in this volume. As a widow, Ellen White turns to her youngest son, Willie, for support.

When she was asked to go to Europe in 1885, she had not received a direct command from God to do so. It wasn't until she sat down in the train in Oakland, California, at the beginning of her trip, that she had the Lord's assurance that she should go. Some church leaders were probably glad for her absence, but the messages did not stop.

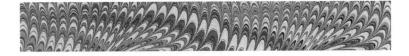

"Brethren of Experience"

5T 289-297

We believe that the Seventh-day Adventist Church has a distinct message to give to the world. Its doctrines have been established by study of the Bible, and prayer, and confirmed through the witness of the modern prophetic gift. But is there more to understand? Can we expect "new light"? Ellen White says so. How should we expect it to come? What guidelines should we follow?

In this chapter, Ellen White deals with a real-life experience in our church more than one hundred years ago, that has implications for us today. A familiar statement from her pen is found in this chapter: "The only safety for any of us is in receiving no new doctrine, no new interpretation of the Scriptures, without first submitting it to brethren of experience. . . If they see no light in it, yield to their judgment"—*Testimonies*, 5:293.

This testimony appeared in May 1885. The recipient, identified only as "Brother D," was William L. Raymond, one of our first ministers in the Oregon and Washington territory.

This is not the first time that Ellen White made the same point. In her first book, published in August 1851, she said: "I saw that the shepherds should consult those in whom they have reason to have confidence, those who have been in all the messages, and are firm in all the present truth, before they advocate new points of importance, which they think the Bible sustains"—*Early Writings*, 61.

In November that year, Ellen White wrote to two ministers who were advocating what they considered "new light": "The messengers of God should be perfectly united in their views of Bible truth and should consult with each other, and should not advance any new view until they first went to the messengers and examined those views with the Bible, and if they were correct, let all the messengers spread them, and if they were error, lay them to one side"—Letter 8, 1861. (See *Ellen G. White, the Early Years*, 221.)

As noted in a previous chapter, Ellen White traveled by ship to Oregon on a "missionary" journey in 1878. She had reported: "My visit to Oregon was one of special interest. I have met, after a separation of four years, my dear friends Brother and Sister Van Horn, whom we claim as our children. I was somewhat surprised, and very much pleased to find the cause of God in so prosperous a condition in Oregon"—*Life Sketches*, 231.

Adelia Patton had lived in the White home for some time before she married Isaac Van Horn. The Van Horns began their work in Washington territory in 1874, fifteen years before it became a state. They held their first baptism in Walla Walla on March 17 of that year. In February 1875, a church was built, and dedicated with a membership of seventy-five. A second church was organized at Milton, Oregon, a few miles away, in January, 1876.

The name of William L. Raymond first appears at the time of Ellen White's 1878 visit in western Oregon. Among other appointments, she attended the first Oregon camp meeting. There, Raymond was ordained to the gospel ministry. He then worked with Van Horn.

Ellen White again visited the North Pacific in 1880. There were three ordained ministers in the territory—I. D. Van Horn, William Raymond, and A. T. Jones (He was later prominent at the 1888 General Conference session). Elder and Mrs. G. W. Colcord joined the ministerial force a few days later.

Two camp meetings were held in 1880, the first at Milton,

Oregon, and the second, east of Portland. Ellen White found that the work of the church was not going nearly as well as at the time of her previous visit. Elder Van Horn was a talented speaker, but his wife and children were requiring more of his time, and his public labor had decreased. He settled west of the Cascade Mountains in Beaverton, Oregon, and had not visited Walla Walla in more than a year, and was not giving strong administrative leadership.

But there were other problems. Ellen White found great prejudice against her. Elder Raymond, now the conference secretary, while very pleasant and humble on the surface, was advancing views out of harmony with what Adventists generally taught. Some of these were on the book of Revelation. He was also very critical of the General Conference. Mrs. White gave strong counsel, both to Van Horn and Raymond. The effect was positive for Van Horn. Mrs. White wrote to her husband: "Elder Van Horn is shaking off his stupor and his testimony has the right ring. He remains president of the conference this side of the Cascades: Brother Colcord, the other side of the Cascades"—Letter 32a, 1880.

Elder Jones was working with Elder Colcord in the new Upper Columbia Conference, and Elder Raymond was working in western Oregon under the direction of Van Horn. Ellen White's counsel to Raymond, however, did not have a lasting effect. He continued to sow seeds of dissension.

Four years later Ellen White again traveled to the Northwest. The counsel she gave at that time is found in several chapters of *Testimonies*, 5:249-302. This study is one of them.

On the 1884 visit, Ellen White spoke at camp meetings at Walla Walla, Washington, and at East Portland, Oregon. By this time the Van Horns had left the area. According to J. N. Loughborough, who accompanied her, Ellen White had her last public vision at the 1884 Portland camp meeting. In his report of the meetings, J. H. Waggoner, editor of the *Signs of the Times* wrote: "Points of doctrine subversive of the message had been introduced, and to some extent been received, which had weakened the faith and courage of many. Reports had also been circulated against most of those who are bearing responsibilities in the work, which caused many to distrust the work itself; and by these means a spirit of complaining had been fostered."

Waggoner then refers to a major source of the trouble: "To no one was the meeting in Walla Walla a greater blessing than to Elder Raymond. He had been somewhat in darkness for some time. In his early experience in this cause he did not receive the instruction which he needed, and he failed to fully realize the nature of the work in the message"—*Signs of the Times*, July 3, 1884.

Elder Raymond was not the only problem, however. Two other men, with little experience, but recognized as ministers, were dropped from the church records because of apostasy at the Portland meeting. Ellen White wrote to S. N. Haskell from the Walla Walla campground: "The enemy is at work through different ones to block the wheels of progress. Elder Raymond has been doing a bad work in complaining of all the leaders and finding fault with the General Conference, the building of churches and schoolhouses. He is a man that can do much harm because he has good traits of character and is of ready tact as a helper"—Letter 19a, 1884.

A few days later, Ellen White wrote to Elder Uriah Smith, author of *Daniel and the Revelation*, a book being sold widely by literature evangelists: "Brother Raymond has never been in harmony with his brethren. He has been independent, self-conceited, but carries such an appearance of humility that nearly all believed him to be the humblest of men. He was talking against the General Conference and finding fault with the men in responsible positions. He had some new light on Revelation; was saying your views on two or three points were incorrect. He was discouraging some from canvassing for *Daniel and Revelation*"—Letter 19, 1884.

What would Ellen White do under these difficult circumstances, when there was such criticism of church leaders? And what would she do when some of the members of the Milton church were running the president (Colcord), and were also trying to tell her what to preach? She wrote, in the same letter to Smith: "We heard them respectfully and preached the Word of the Lord without any reference to their suggestions."

She continued: "Just as soon as we preached the plain principles of truth there was a buzzing in camp like a swarm of bees. They said Elder Waggoner and I were clubbing them. They did not want that kind of preaching."

Then she said: "I can tell you there was great astonishment and marveling that I dared to speak to them thus. . . . Brother Raymond was going to go right away from the camp. He said we were clubbing him."

Then, note the short, crisp language she uses: "I sent for him. I read to him. I talked with him. I told him that when my brethren, as did Brother Owen, come up with new light . . . I knew it was a device of Satan which no one could understand although a man declare it unto them"—ibid. The result of the confrontation was that Elder Raymond was helped. He submitted his views to a council of the brethren, and they wrote out their answer, which he accepted.

In a letter to Smith, a few days later, Ellen White looks down to our day, and offers reasons for preserving this experience: "From that which the Lord has been pleased to show me there will arise just such ones all along, and many more of them claiming to have new light which is a side issue, an entering wedge. The widening will increase until there is a breach made between those who accept these views and those who believe the third angel's message. Just as soon as these new ideas are accepted, then there will be a drawing away from those whom God has used in this work, for the mind begins to doubt and withdraw from the leaders because God has laid them aside and chosen more humble men to do His work. This is the only interpretation they can give to this matter, as the leaders do not see this important 'light.' "

Continuing in the same letter, she says: "It is Satan's object now to get up new theories to divert the mind from the true work and genuine message for this time. He stirs up minds to give false interpretation of Scripture, a spurious loud cry, that the real message will not have its effect when it does come." (Quoted in *Manuscript Releases,* 9:27.)

Ellen White stood strongly behind her testimonies. She knew their Source. After this hard work, she could say: "The only thing they did not dare to reject was the testimonies"—Letter 20, 1884. Unfortunately, this is not always the case.

Mrs. White was pointed in her concerns expressed for Raymond: "He is not correct in all points of doctrine." "He obstinately maintains his erroneous positions." "He is an accuser of the brethren." "He has not only thought evil, but spoken evil to others." He has not . . . conferred with the leading brethren, and yet he finds fault with them all"—*Testimonies*, 5:289.

Elder Raymond opposed Ellen White's testimonies: "Suppose that Brother D (Raymond) leads the people to question and reject the testimonies that God has been giving to His people during the past thirty-eight years; suppose he makes them believe that the leaders in this work are designing, dishonest men, engaged in deceiving the people; what great and good work has he done?" (290).

A good question—still today!

This is not a very positive picture of one of the few ministers in a territory. Ellen White goes on to compare Raymond's tactics to those of Satan, who "represented that God had done him injustice in preferring Christ to himself."

Mrs. White then makes a very significant point about those who claim to have new light: "God has not passed His people by and chosen one solitary man here and another there as the only ones worthy to be entrusted with His truth. He does not give one man new light contrary to the established faith of the body" (291).

She made this same point in 1858, when someone was urging that giving up swine's flesh should be made a test. She wrote: "If it is the duty of the church to abstain from swine's flesh, God will discover it to more than two or three. He will teach His *church* their duty"—*Testimonies*, 1:207.

In the chapter we are studying, Ellen White offers a classic understanding of how false "new light" develops. First, it is "apparently harmless." Then, the "original idea. . . does not seem to conflict with the truth." Next, "He talks of it and dwells upon it until it seems to him to be clothed with beauty and importance." Eventually "it becomes the all-absorbing theme, the one great point around which everything centers." At last, "the truth is uprooted from the heart" (292).

She then considers several other tactics of Satan: "Satan will rush in many errors to divert the mind from the importance of the truth for this time" (292). He is "noiseless," "stealthy," "masked," and "not open." He and "his agents act in concert. A line of unbelief stretches across the continent and is in communication with the church of God." "Men and women," under his influence, "will arise professing to have some new light or some new revelation whose tendency is to unsettle faith in the old landmarks" (294-296).

It is clear, then, that genuine new light does not destroy old light!

In speaking of men like Raymond, Ellen White says that Satan "fills them with notions of their own sufficiency, and persuades them . . . that originality is a gift much to be coveted" (296). More important than originality, she says, "Brother D [Raymond] needs to learn the truth more perfectly" (296).

Ellen White later spoke about the danger of seeking to be original: "Some zealous ones who are aiming and straining every energy for originality have made a grave mistake in trying to get something startling, wonderful, entrancing before the people, something that they think others do not comprehend; but they do not themselves know what they are talking about"—*Selected Messages*, 1:180.

In still another place she writes: "As we take up the study of God's word, we should do so with humble hearts. All selfishness, all love of originality, should be laid aside. . . . Those who sincerely desire truth will not be reluctant to lay open their positions for investigation and criticism, and will not be annoyed if their opinions and ideas are crossed"—*Review*, July 26, 1892. (See *Counsels to Writers and Editors*, 36, 37.)

William L. Raymond dropped out of the ministerial records in 1887. Ironically, perhaps, it was the same year that another prominent minister left the church—D. M. Canright.

God Spoke to Me This Way

5T 654-691

Ellen White compiled this chapter in 1889, shortly after the historic 1888 General Conference at Minneapolis, Minnesota, where the subject of righteousness by faith was presented by A. T. Jones and E. J. Waggoner. Their message was opposed by some prominent church leaders, as history can testify. Because she supported Jones and Waggoner, some of these same church leaders began to question her inspiration. A major opponent was no other than Uriah Smith, a close associate and friend for many years.

The counsel she gave to Smith at this time was perhaps as strong as any given during her prophetic ministry. She rather pointedly reminded Smith that he had abundant evidence of her divine calling, and his attitude was affecting others and seriously undermining her work. He surely must have read this chapter in the *Testimonies* volumes with special interest.

At this same time, D. M. Canright, a former Seventh-day Adventist minister, was offering his strongest opposition to her work, charging her with plagiarism. An introduction to *The Great Controversy*, written by Ellen White, was first included in the 1888 edition of the book. In this introduction, she states why she quoted other authors and why she did not always give credit to them: "In some cases where a historian has so grouped together events as to afford, in brief, a comprehensive view of the subject, or has summarized details in a convenient manner, his words have been quoted; but in some instances no specific credit has been given, since the quotations are not given for the purpose of citing that writer as authority, but because his statement affords a ready and forcible presentation of the subject"—*The Great Controversy*, Intro., xi,xii.

Mrs. White rarely chose to defend herself and her ministry. But both in *The Great Controversy* Introduction, and in this compilation, she took the initiative to explain how she understood her work. Gathering material from earlier volumes of *Testimonies*, and including additional comments, she spoke of what God had shown her in four different ways: (1) The "nature" and (2) "importance" of the testimonies, (3) "the manner in which they are given," and (4) "how they should be regarded" (654).

Beginning on a personal level, she tells of her call to the prophetic ministry as a seventeen-year-old. The angel who spoke to her in vision, promised that God would save her from pride by bringing "affliction." Surely some of her illness through her life accomplished this purpose. But immediately after the 1844 disappointment, there were "serious errors in doctrine and practice, and some were ready to condemn all who would not accept their views" (655). These problems occupied her first attention. Her visions required her to show these people their errors. It should not be surprising that she was met with "bitter opposition."

Under these circumstances she decided to observe reactions, and then "soften" her correction if there was resistance. But after so doing, feelings of guilt swept across her, and she wished for death. Then, in vision she was taken into "the presence of Jesus." He frowned at her and turned away. She was devastated. She imagined it like being among those who are finally lost, as they are rejected by Christ.

But the vision was not over. A group of people to whom she had given messages crowded around her. They had torn clothes and disheveled hair and as they rubbed against her, there was blood on her clothing. It was a symbol of her responsibility if they would be lost—"blood on her garments." The angel said that this had not happened yet but that she should give the counsel just as given to her, with no changes to suit those who objected.

Soon after this, she had a dream in which she was told to cut out garments of all sizes. It was made clear that this symbol represented her giving of testimonies to a variety of people. She was to do her work, leaving the results with God: "In rebuking the wrongs of one, He [God] designs to correct many" (659).

Ellen White repeatedly speaks of two parts to the work that God had given her. Here she speaks of them as "warnings and judgments," and "the sweet promise of mercy." Later, in this chapter she mentions "reproof" and "encouragement" (687). Still earlier in her ministry, she spoke of her role as giving "correction" and "comfort"—*Early Writings*, 78.

These are reminders that there are always two sides to the work of God's messengers, whether they be prophets or preachers, or even friends. Mercy and love and forgiveness must always be extended to the sinner. Repeatedly this principle is found in the Bible and in the writings of Ellen White.

Instead of replacing the Bible, she presents her writing as bringing us back to it, calling attention to its principles, impressing truth already given, and encouraging use of the light given. This phase of her work was also repeatedly demonstrated, beginning with the first study of doctrines in the middle 1840s. Ellen White's visions did not occur to take the place of Scripture study, but to support it, giving understanding of it. James White speaks about how her contemporaries accepted this role: "The revival of any, or of all the Gifts, will never supercede the necessity of searching the Word to learn the truth. . . . It is not God's plan to lead out His people into the broad field of truth by the gifts. But after his people have searched the Word, if then individuals err from Bible truth, or through strife urge erroneous views upon the honest seekers for truth, then is God's opportunity to correct them by the Gifts. This is in harmony with our entire experience on this subject."—*Review*, February 28, 1856. (See also *Testimonies*, 1: 713, 714.)

Ellen White reminds her readers that the ceremonies of the Old Testament were necessary only because the people were not obeying God's law. She implies that her special testimonies would not have been necessary if God's people had been following God's Word as they should have. (See 5T:665). Writing in 1862, she had said that the testimonies should not be unduly urged upon two classes of people:

1. Those "who have never seen the individual having visions."

2. Those "who have had no personal knowledge of the influence of the visions" (668).

But there is the other side. If some fight against the visions of which they have no knowledge, or oppose that in which they have no experience, then, she said, "the church may know that they are not right" (669).

She urges other cautions: not to use the visions when talking to unbelievers, or as an iron rule for others, while ignoring them ourselves, or taking an extreme meaning of the counsel. Her cautions, elsewhere, on extreme positions is especially significant. Ellen White's writing, rightly understood, is balanced and reasonable.

Attitudes toward the work of God's messenger do make a difference. A sequence is suggested: (1) Jealousy of leaders. (2) Next, questioning the gifts of the Spirit. (3) Then, disregarding instruction from vision. (4) This is followed by skepticism on vital points of faith. (5) Then comes doubt of the Bible. (6) Finally, a "downward march to perdition" (672).

Some wrong attitudes to the "Testimonies" are enumerated: (672, 673)

1. Talking flippantly about them
2. Passing judgment on them
3. Criticizing this and that
4. Taking a course of their own choosing
5. Putting false construction on them
6. Suggesting they are unreliable

7. They are uncalled for

8. It is a mark of intelligence to doubt

9. Turning away because there are a few things not understood

She was asked by God to treat friends and foes alike. This requirement was often dramatic. We have already noted reproof to Uriah Smith and D. M. Canright. Both of these men were close friends.Her special connection with John Harvey Kellogg began earlier in his medical work. She had promised his parents that she would stay by him as long as she could. But, finally, there came a time when she had to write boldly and plainly that he was wrong.

There was also the unpremeditated counsel. When the Bushnell, Michigan, church was dwindling in membership, they voted to close down. Ellen White visited there personally, and publicly pointed out individual problems. There was confession of wrong, and the church stayed open.

In the winter of 1867, Ellen White, with her husband, and J. N. Andrews, participated in a revival in the Washington, New Hampshire, church. There she gave *public* correction to a respected church leader, William Farnsworth, one of the first Sabbath keepers. He was secretly using tobacco. After these meetings, eighteen young people were baptized, more than half of which later gave their lives in service for the church, including Farnsworth's son, Eugene.

Ellen White's work was sometimes made more difficult by those who showed what she called "unsanctified sympathy" with persons who had been corrected. She clearly saw this attitude as limiting the usefulness of her counsel. She spoke about her call to do such work: "I have not chosen this unpleasant labor for myself," she said (679). This was true of all prophets.

Thirty years after she had begun her ministry, she still found it a difficult responsibility. Writing to J. N. Loughborough, in 1874, she confessed: "I have felt for years that if I could have my choice and please God as well, I would rather die than have a vision. For every vision places me under great responsibility to bear messages of correction. Never have I coveted my position, yet I dare not resist the Spirit of God, and seek an easier position"—*Selected Messages*, 3:36, 37.

There are many ways people try to avoid responsibilities. But one of the most common is neglect. If we don't read the Bible, it cannot affect our lives. The same is true of the counsel through the prophetic voice in the advent movement. Truth that does not save us, hardens us. It can even be shown that some Bible reading is positively harmful—the reading that we refuse to heed (681).

If we believe, indeed, that God speaks through visions to prophets. And when we have tested the prophet and found them to be genuine, then their message tests us. We must believe that God has spoken, not a mere human.

It is not our place to pick and choose what we will believe or accept. When we do this, we become our own internal authority. Throughout history, when God has given messages through His prophets, those who have accepted have been blessed. Those who have not accepted, have failed. Some have tried to rationalize away the importance and authority of what has been spoken or written. Ellen White observes some of these wrong tactics:

1. If a vision is not for me personally, then it is of no more value than any other message.

2. It is a message influenced by others.

3. It is merely private judgment.

4. It was only given in response to another person.

5. We might be tempted to pick and choose. (ibid., 653, 684.)

It is obvious that some church leaders questioned the authority of Ellen White's messages. To such, she said: "If you, my brethren, who have been acquainted with me and my work for many years, take the position that my counsel is of no more value than the counsel of those who have not been specially educated for this work, then do not ask me to unite with you in labor; for while you occupy this position, you will inevitably counteract the influence of my work" (688).

She suggests that doubt can become a way of life: "Those who train the mind to seize upon everything which they can use as a peg to hang a doubt upon, and suggest these thoughts to other minds, will always find occasion to doubt" (690).

But she makes an even more startling statement about those who question and criticize everything and everybody who does not believe exactly like themselves: "They will feed upon the errors and mistakes and faults of others, 'until,' said the angel, 'the Lord Jesus shall rise up from His mediatorial work in the heavenly sanctuary and shall clothe Himself with the garments of vengeance and surprise them at their unholy feast, and they will find themselves unprepared for the marriage of the lamb.' " But the statement even gets more incredible. Ellen White continues: "Their taste has been so perverted that they would be inclined to criticize even the table of the Lord in His kingdom" (690).

In this chapter, Ellen White goes back to a statement she made in 1873: "Those who desire to doubt will have plenty of room. God does not propose to remove all occasion for unbelief. He gives evidence, which must be carefully investigated with a humble mind and a teachable spirit, and *all should decide from the weight of evidence*" (657, emphasis supplied).

It is clear that God does not answer every question. In fact, the statement above suggests that He does it on purpose, to test us. But it is equally clear that He provides enough evidence on which to base belief. Faith is not a blind thing, but rather "the substance of things hoped for, the evidence of things not seen"—Hebrews 11:1.

There is one other thing. It may seem, on the surface, that Ellen White's positive statements about her work and messages are egotistical. But there is a common attitude shared by Ellen White and Bible writers. They were humble about themselves, but very positive and sure of their messages. Paul spoke of himself as the "chief of sinners," but also encouraged others to accept his message as from the Lord. Ellen White did the same. She wrote at the conclusion of this chapter: "I have no special wisdom in myself; I am only an instrument In the Lord's hands to do the work He has set for me to do. The instructions that I have given by pen or voice have been an expression of the light that God has given me" (691).

Introduction to Volume 6

1891-1900

This volume encompasses the nine years that Ellen White was in Australia and New Zealand. She was sixty-three years of age when she went, and seventy-two when she returned to America. No retirement time for this prophet! This is the first volume to be arranged topically, published all at one time, rather than in segments, as earlier volumes were.

The Pitcairn, a missionary sailing ship, had been launched in 1890. Many colleges, sanitariums and publishing houses were established in this time.

Several books were also completed by Ellen White during these years. They were *Steps to Christ* and *Gospel Workers*, in 1892; *Christian Education*, in 1893; *Thoughts From the Mount of Blessing*, in 1896; *The Desire of Ages*, in 1898; and *Christ's Object Lessons* and *Testimonies*, volume 6, in 1900.

When she arrived in Australia, Ellen White began calling for a college, even though there were only about five hundred church members. The possibility seemed remote. But her message went even further. The college, she said, should be built on a large piece of land. On a train trip to look at the property, it was remarked: "It seems strange to be looking for a large piece of land, when we hardly have enough money to pay the train fare to go and look at it." But 1,500 acres were found at a bargain price of three dollars an acre, and a friend of Ellen White loaned the money to buy it.

As a small group of about thirty people gathered to watch Ellen White lay the cornerstone for Bethel Hall, it was a pretty sober crowd. She looked around, and said, with a smile: "Cheer up children. This is a resurrection, not a funeral." She then proceeded with the ceremony.

Speaking the Truth in Love

6T 120-123

This chapter is an example of compilation work directed by Ellen White herself. Her last will and testament stipulated that she wanted compiling to continue after her death. As a result, scores of books have been published and are a blessing to the church as this work has continued. The material in this short chapter was compiled from seven different sources.

The first five paragraphs are taken from the *Review*, July 14, 1896; the next paragraph is from Letter 59, 1900, to A. T. Jones; the next paragraph is also from a letter to Jones, Letter 17, 1900; the next paragraph is from Manuscript 64, 1894; the next from Letter 13, 1897; the next four paragraphs are taken from Letter 91, 1899, also to Jones; and the final paragraph is from Manuscript 16, 1890. In this study, we will concentrate on those portions written to A. T. Jones. But first, let's get briefly acquainted with him.

Alonzo T. Jones came into the Seventh-day Adventist Church from an army background. He was baptized in Walla Walla, Washington Territory, August 8, 1874, at the age of twenty-four. His first sermon was delivered soon after his baptism. In his early ministerial work in the North Pacific area, he teamed with Elder I. D. Van Horn, and a third minister, William L. Raymond. We studied about him in an earlier chapter. These three men were the entire working force in the area then.

When Mrs. White traveled to the northwest in 1878, and again in 1880, she saw great potential in Jones as a minister. Raymond was critical of the church and its leadership, and did not understand Adventist belief fully. His fault-finding toward church leaders no doubt had some influence on Jones, who later was also critical of the church, its organization and leadership. In 1887, Raymond left the Adventist ministry in apostasy. Jones would follow along in apostasy at a later time.

After ten years in the ministry in the Northwest, Jones transferred to northern California in 1884. He assisted in editorial work on *Signs of the Times* and the *Sabbath Sentinel*, our religious liberty journal. Ellet J. Waggoner also did editorial work on these two journals at the same time. It was the beginning of their close association, eventually leading up to their presentations in Minneapolis in 1888. Jones' articles began appearing in the *Review* early in 1884. In the fall of 1885, he taught Bible at Healdsburg College, along with his editorial work. He later was pastor of the Healdsburg church. His ministry was very successful, and by 1887, he had become a leading minister on the west coast.

In Battle Creek, George I. Butler, president of the General Conference, and Uriah Smith, editor of the *Review*, represented the older generation of leadership, while Jones and Waggoner represented the younger. These young men, through the pages of the *Signs*, began to challenge some interpretations of Scripture, and the prophecies of Daniel—positions held by Smith and most Adventists. This challenge provided the backdrop for a major confrontation at the 1888 General Conference session in Minneapolis. The conflict revolved around several issues. They included (1) a pending national Sunday law; (2) identity of the law in Galatians; (3) who the ten kingdoms in Daniel 7 were; (4) claims of a "California conspiracy" including Jones, Waggoner, and Ellen White, to change doctrinal positions in the church; and, finally, (5) the personalities of the participants.

The conflict began at the ministerial institute held October 10-19, and carried over into the business session that followed. On several occasions, in the institute, Jones publicly attacked the prophetic interpretations of Uriah Smith. His comments were often sharp and harsh. W. C. White, Ellen White's son, spoke of the "pomposity and egotism" of both Jones and Waggoner. Mrs. White cautioned Jones especially, on several occasions, in following years, about his public presentations. These concerns are reflected in this chapter.

There is no question that Jones and Waggoner were used by the Lord in presenting a subject that urgently needed to be given. Their message on righteousness by faith was a powerful one. And Ellen White supported it. In so doing, she placed herself at odds with George Butler and Uriah Smith, among others. These men had been her strong allies for many years.

Following the session, she traveled with Jones and Waggoner as they presented righteousness by faith. For the next several years, they were featured speakers at General Conference sessions, ministerial meetings, and camp meetings all across the United States. Gradually, righteousness by faith was accepted by most Adventists. But Ellen White's greater concern seemed to be for the contentious spirit displayed by the combatants at Minneapolis, and long afterwards by some. She spoke of it as "so unlike the spirit of Jesus," and more like the Pharisees.

Because Mrs. White came to the defense of Jones and Waggoner, her own inspiration was questioned by some of her closest associates. During the years following, she wrote some of her strongest letters of rebuke to Butler and Smith for their attitudes. At the same time, she did not waver in her support of the renewed emphasis on Christ and His righteousness. Writing to O. A. Olsen, president of the General Conference, in 1895, she said:

"The Lord in His great mercy sent a most precious message to His people through Elders Waggoner and Jones. This message was to bring more prominently before the world the uplifted Saviour, the sacrifice for the sins of the whole world. It presented justification through faith in the Surety; it invited the people to receive the righteousness of Christ, which is made manifest in obedience to all the commandments of God. Many had lost sight of Jesus. They needed to have their eyes directed to His divine person, His merits, and His changeless love for the human family"—Letter 57, 1895 (see *Testimonies to Ministers*, 91, 92).

But she also had some strong counsel for Jones. His public presentations sometimes were unloving and tactless. She said that the way he spoke was often misunderstood by his audiences. He frequently used overstatement to make a point. Writing to him on April 9, 1893, she tells of a dream in which she listened to his preaching: "I was attending a meeting and a large congregation were present. In my dream you were presenting the subject of faith and the imputed righteousness of Christ by faith. You repeated several times that works amounted to nothing, that there were no conditions. The matter was presented in that light and I knew that minds would be confused, and would not receive the correct impression in reference to faith and works, and I decided to write to you.

"You state this matter too strongly. There are conditions to our receiving justification and sanctification, and the righteousness of Christ. I know your meaning, but you leave a wrong impression upon many minds."

Then she says: "While good works will not save even one soul, yet it is impossible for even one soul to be saved without good works."

She then refers to the young man who came to Jesus, asking "Good Master, what good thing shall I do, that I may have eternal life?" Jesus pointed him to the commandments. When the young man declared that he had kept all of the commandments, Jesus asked him to "sell that thou hast, and give to the poor, and thou shalt have treasure in heaven; come and follow me."

Ellen White then emphatically states: "Here are conditions, and the Bible is full of conditions."

She continues: "When you say there are no conditions, and

some expressions are made quite broad, you burden the minds, and some cannot see the consistency in your expressions. They cannot see how they can harmonize these expressions with the plain statements of the Word of God."

As she concludes her letter, she comments on 2 Peter 1:1-11 as follows: "This is the faith which we must have, that works by love, and purifies the soul. There is no place in the school of Christ where we graduate. We are to work on the plan of addition, and the Lord will work on the plan of multiplication"—Letter 44, 1893 (quoted in *The 1888 Materials*, 1164-1166).

In 1894, Jones joined with another church leader, W. W. Prescott, in extolling Anna Phillips, a young lady who claimed to have the prophetic gift. These men publicly endorsed her so-called visions, sometimes comparing them with the visions of Ellen White. Mrs. White wrote to these two men from Australia in 1894, warning them that Anna's messages were not from the Lord.

Prescott and Jones gave up their support for Anna Phillips, and Anna herself surrendered her claims. In her letter to Prescott and Jones, Ellen White made a powerful statement about attempting to create feeling that still has implications today:

"If we work to create an excitement of feeling, we shall have all we want, and more than we can possibly know how to manage. Calmly and clearly 'preach the word.' We must not regard it as our work to create an excitement. The Holy Spirit of God alone can create a healthy enthusiasm"—Letter 68, 1894 (quoted in *Selected Messages*, 2:95).

Writing to Jones in 1902, Mrs. White used a parable to characterize his preaching style: "Your work has been represented to me in figures. You were passing round to a company a vessel filled with the most beautiful fruit. But as you offered them this fruit, you spoke words so harsh, and your attitude was so forbidding, that no one would accept it. Then another came to the same company, and offered them the same fruit. And so courteous and pleasant were His words and the manner as He spoke of the desirability of the fruit, that the vessel was emptied"—Letter 164, 1902 (see ibid., 3:44, 45).

If we are to understand all of the circumstances in 1888, however, we must look at how the older generation had come to this point in time. From the beginning, Adventists who survived the 1844 disappointment frequently focused on their differences from the rest of the religious world. They often defended their reason to exist. From the beginning, the heart of their message was usually the law of God. And the Sabbath was its central commandment.

Early visions given to Ellen White in 1846 and 1847 seemed to support this approach. She saw the heavenly sanctuary, with Christ was ministering in the most holy place as our High Priest. She also saw the commandments in the ark, and observed that there was a halo of light surrounding the Sabbath commandment. This was considered evidence of its special importance.

The first paper published by James White, *The Present Truth*, is interesting in this connection. Every article in that first eight-page issue of July 1849, spoke either about the law or the Sabbath. Joseph Bates' earliest pamphlet, in 1846, was also on the subject of the Sabbath. J. N. Andrews also developed the Sabbath theme in a more detailed defense in several editions of his book, *History of the Sabbath*. Uriah Smith, a prolific writer and editor of the *Review* for nearly fifty years, often dealt with the law and the Sabbath through its pages.

Attention to the law became so central, however, that Christ was lost sight of by many Adventists. More balance was needed between the law and righteousness by faith. Looking back to 1888 and earlier, Ellen White spoke about the problem in a sermon on February 6, 1890: "As a people, we have preached the law until we are as dry as the hills of Gilboa, that had neither dew nor rain. We must preach Christ in the law, and there will be sap and nourishment in the preaching that will be as food to the famishing flock of God"—*Review*, March 11, 1890.

And so, this was the setting for controversy at the 1888 General Conference session. But let's look at what Mrs. White wrote to Jones in this chapter of volume 6:

"Follow other methods than that of condemning wrong, even

though the condemnation be just . . . Do something more than to hurl at . . . adversaries charges that only drive them further from the truth" (121).

"The influence of your teaching would be tenfold greater if you were careful of your words. . . .If by your spirit or your words you close the door to even one soul, that soul will confront you in the judgment. . . . Do not, when referring to the *Testimonies*, feel it your duty to drive them home" (122).

She further warned about his public reading of the *Testimonies*: "Be sure not to mix in your filling of words, for this makes it impossible for the hearers to distinguish between the word of the Lord to them and your words."

She continues her caution: "Every sermon you preach, every article you write, may be all true; but one drop of gall in it will be poison to the hearer or the reader."

"Another," she said, "will feed on the poison; for he loves such harsh words; he follows your example, and talks just as you talk. Thus the evil is multiplied" (122, 123).

The entire contents of Letter 91, 1899, from which four paragraphs on pages 122 and 123 of this volume are taken can be read in *Manuscript Releases*, 19:195-200. The following are further extracts from this letter:

"Whoever edits the *Sentinel* [Jones] needs to have his pen dipped in holy oil, that the words traced shall not reveal a sharp, thrusting, warfaring spirit. The Lord would have you, my brother, mellow up and not be harsh and overbearing. You hurt yourself when you are rash and impetuous."

"My brother Jones, you need the subduing influence of the Spirit of God. You have hereditary traits of character that are constantly striving for the supremacy."

"Brother Jones, be careful in your words. You know the truth, and I urge you for Christ's sake to practice the truth. . . . You need the spirit of meekness and gentleness, of patience and forbearance, and of love for your brethren."

"Make it your aim to speak the truth in love. Then the Lord

Jesus by His Spirit will supply the force and the power. That is the Lord's work. Beware lest with the sacred you mingle the common fire—A. T. Jones—in your service. Your common utterances are as common fire in the service of God. We must not mingle self with anything we do for God."

It is quite clear that there were wrong attitudes on both sides of the debate that went on at Minneapolis. George Butler and Uriah Smith later confessed their wrong positions and attitudes. Jones, however, in later years continued his harsh criticism of the church, its organization, and leaders, until he left it in apostasy. What a tragic story it is. A man who was so powerfully used in bringing the message of righteousness by faith to the Seventh-day Adventist Church did not continue to the end. E. J. Waggoner later left the church as well.

Obviously, Jones was unable to apply the message in a practical way to his own life, so that he might continue to bear fruit to the glory of God. His ministerial credentials were taken from him in 1907, and he was disfellowshipped from the Seventh-day Adventist Church in 1909. He died on May 12, 1923.

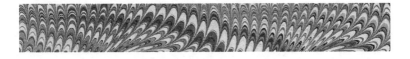

The Haskell Home for Orphans

6T 281-287

Care of orphans was not an early priority of the Seventh-day Adventist Church. In fact, it was about the last type of institution that was established among us. Early in our history, we built publishing houses, schools, and medical facilities. But actually, the subject was a concern of Ellen White from soon after the church was formally organized.

The beginning of our orphanages is stated as follows: "The first systematic effort of Seventh-day Adventists to provide for orphan and destitute children had its inception at the meeting of the General Conference held in the spring of 1891."—*Year Book of the Seventh-day Adventist Medical Missionary and Benevolent Association*, 1866-1896, 82.

Doctor and Mrs. John Harvey Kellogg for many years cared for orphan children in their home. They had no children of their own. But after some time it became evident that they could no longer keep up with the demand. After Kellogg talked with Ellen White about an orphan home, she wrote, on October 16, 1890: "To the Managers of the Battle Creek Sanitarium—Dear Brethren: While in Petosky I had some conversation with your physician in chief in regard to establishing a home for orphan children at Battle Creek. I said that this was just what was needed among us as a people, and that in enterprises of this kind we were far behind other denominations"—*Testimonies*, 8:133.

Kellogg circulated this encouragement for an orphan's home, and at his urging, the 1891 General Conference session at Battle Creek, voted authorization for such an institution. He suggested that it be called "The James White Memorial Home."

But Kellogg did not emphasize certain warnings Ellen White had stated in her letter. She had said: "To plan largely for Battle Creek is not wise. The world is our field of labor, and the money expended in this one place would go far toward carrying forward successful aggressive work in other places"—ibid., 135.

She also said: "There is need that institutions be established in different places, that men and women may be set at work to do their best in the fear of God"—ibid., 137.

Writing later, Mrs. White continued to speak about the type of institution needed for orphans: "Such institutions to be most effective, should be modeled as closely as possible after the plan of a Christian home. Instead of large establishments, bringing great numbers together, let there be small institutions in different places"—*The Ministry of Healing*, 205.

"Such institutions," she said, "should be in the country, where land might be cultivated, the children brought into contact with nature, and where they could have industrial training"—ibid., 205, 206. Many of these concepts were carried out in Battle Creek. The church did establish orphanages in several countries in following years.

Kellogg set about the raising of money for the orphanage, estimating the cost at $50,000. But he found out that it was not easy to raise the necessary funds. After one year of work, he had raised only $20,000 of the projected cost. As soon as it was known that an orphanage was planned, however, applications began to come in. And children began to arrive too. They were put in small cottages at first, but it was evident that more space was needed.

Then, in April 1892, from a totally unexpected source, Kellogg found the money needed. Caroline Haskell, a Presbyterian guest at the Sanitarium, who had admired his work with orphaned children, talked with Kellogg about her desire to support him. He told her of his plans for an orphanage, and she donated $30,000 from the estate of her late husband, Frederick Haskell, stipulating that it be named "The Haskell Home." This was agreed upon, and now Kellogg had the money necessary to complete the project. Of course, he built it in Battle Creek. It was probably one of the few projects that Doctor Kellogg was associated with, that was debt-free from the start.

The orphanage was dedicated on January 25, 1894, at a cost of $52,870. It opened with forty children and five caretakers. Three years later, there were ninety-five residents. At its height, as many as two hundred children were cared for at one time.

As a special feature of the management of the building, the children were grouped into families of about twelve, each under the direction of a qualified woman, or "mother." Each "family" had its own suite, with a sitting room, a dormitory for sleeping, a mother's room, and clothes room. The children all ate in one dining hall, but each family had its own table and chairs. Older boys, with a "father," were grouped together.

The children attended school each weekday four or five hours. Special attention was given to their diet, dress, posture, and religious training, along with a physical exercise program. The older children worked daily at manual labor on the farm, in the garden, or in domestic duties. Training in gymnastics was also included. Some children were adopted from the Home into Adventist families, but many stayed until their late teens.

Every day's schedule began at 6:00 a.m., with all rising except the infants. Morning worship was held in the chapel from 6:45 to 7:45. From 1:00 to 2:00 p.m. devotional meetings were held for the adult members of the staff, and each family had worship in their own rooms before bedtime.

The Home was located on a 67-acre farm, and was operated

on a donation basis. The farm included 12,000 peach trees, 1,000 plum trees, 300 pear trees, and several hundred apple trees. There was a vineyard, strawberries, raspberries, and blackberries. There were also currants and gooseberries. Some of the produce was sold, but most was used by the Home.

In 1897, a special magazine, *The Haskell Home Appeal*, was begun to help raise funds for the home. *The Medical Missionary* magazine also encouraged financial support. Semiannual offerings were taken in Adventist churches.

This chapter in *Testimonies for the Church* was written while Ellen White was in Australia, and at about the time that the Haskell Home was opened. But it was not the first, nor the last time, that she wrote on the subject. For many years, she had urged that orphans should not be neglected by the church. She herself kept orphan children in her home, during her long ministry. She spoke of this: "Although called to travel often, and having much writing to do, I have taken children of three and five years of age, and have cared for them, educated them, and trained them for responsible positions. I have taken into my home from time to time boys from ten to sixteen years of age, giving them motherly care, and training for service"—*Selected Messages*, 1:34.

Her first mention of such a need goes back as early as 1869, when she wrote about duty to orphans in *Testimonies*. She wrote again on the subject in 1875 (see Ibid., 3:511-521). A collection of several of her statements can be found in *Welfare Ministry*, 220-231. She also spoke of the need of care for orphans in Australia, while she was there (see *Life Sketches*, 349-378). On several occasions she wrote about orphans in Adventist periodicals.

Why was there such a need at that time? Several reasons can be found. It was a period of very high mortality rates for all ages. With so many early deaths, the average life expectancy was only in the middle thirties. Widespread epidemics often wiped out most members of a family. Mothers often died giving birth to children, tuberculosis was almost unchecked, and the Civil War brought death to many fathers. There were thousands of orphans who needed to be cared for.

The great champion of orphans, George Mueller, preceded our work for orphans, in England. Beginning in 1836, he established a number of orphanages, finally caring for many thousands. He died in 1898, at the age of ninety-two, and his legacy in this work is well known.

We might ask why there are no longer large orphanages such as Mueller built in Bristol, England. And why are there few Adventist orphanages today? It is a different world today. There are other ways to provide, and advanced knowledge in care for the sick has dramatically improved life expectancy.

After Ellen White visited the Haskell Home in 1901, she wrote to Kellogg: "I was much pleased with my visit to the orphan's home. I feel so thankful that the homeless can have so pleasant a home. I have never before seen gathered together so large a number of children, and all so bright and cheerful. Their faces are healthy, their eyes clear, their nerves strong. To see them and hear them does me more good than a dose of medicine. . . . This home is an educating school for both boys and girls. If I had children whom I would be compelled to leave motherless, I would feel it a great privilege to leave them in such a home"—Letter 70, 1901.

But the Haskell Home suffered a fate similar to other Adventist institutions in Battle Creek. It was destroyed by fire on February 5, 1909. At the time of the fire, there were only thirty-seven residents as compared to much larger numbers at its height. Three children died in the fire. It was the last major fire, of more than a dozen that had affected our institutions in that city, from 1887 to 1909.

Mrs. White's warning that she saw fires destroying the buildings in Battle Creek were well known there, not only by Adventists, but by the community. The Battle Creek *Daily Moon* had extensive comment on the fire, suggesting that "Battle Creek will hesitate to believe any other theory than that the building was deliberately set a fire by fanatics anxious to make Mother White's prophecies that Battle Creek will be destroyed by fire come true"—ibid.

The *Daily Moon* reported that "the cause of the fire is shrouded in mystery—and a mystery which arouses strange fears in the minds of citizens who recall the many disastrous fires which have visited so many of the institutions in the West End and the causes of which are still unexplained"—February 5, 1909.

The papers reported that the Haskell Home was no longer directly connected with the Seventh-day Adventist Church, because of conflict between Doctor Kellogg and Ellen White. From 1906, the denomination had ceased solicited funds for the Home. By this time, Kellogg had separated from the church. He rebuilt the Haskell Home on a much smaller scale, but finally closed its doors in 1922.

At the same time that care for orphans was being considered, a home for the aged was proposed. Mrs. Haskell's gift temporarily diverted interest from this project. In late 1894, Doctor Kellogg offered the use of two houses he owned, and the Medical Missionary Benevolent Association operated the buildings provided, under the name of "The James White Memorial Home." Finally, a three-story house was built that could care for forty people. In 1920, Kellogg transferred the James White Memorial Home to the Lake Union Conference of Seventh-day Adventists.

In his earliest years at Battle Creek Sanitarium, Kellogg made it a witness for the church. As time went by, however, he concentrated his energies more on medical lines. He finally changed the title of his organization to "The International Medical Missionary Benevolent Association," leaving out all mention of the church. This represented more than a change of name, as he developed the nondenominational character of his work.

Kellogg also began focusing more and more on the Chicago slums, with little or no emphasis on the gospel. Mrs. White warned that he was making such work the whole body of the message. Writing to the Battle Creek Sanitarium Board, January 2, 1898, she said: "As the right arm is to the body, so is the medical missionary work to the third angel's message. But the right arm is not to become the whole body. The work of seeking the outcasts is important, but it is not to become the great burden of our mission"—Letter 2, 1898.

While she was in Australia, Ellen White wrote repeatedly that the poor should not be neglected, for she did some of this work herself. She wrote to Kellogg of her practices: "I thought of what we had done and were doing here to help the poor, to lift up the bowed down and oppressed, to clothe the naked and feed the hungry, all of whom were just as precious in the sight of the Lord as the same class in America. In a variety of ways we were carrying on the very work that you are doing, but we had not numerous churches to draw upon."

She helped one man to pay for a home. Another was advanced money to pay rent. To another she loaned a cow. She also took the sick into her home. Then she said to Kellogg: "But it is not our duty to let all the Lord's money to flow in these channels. There is sacred, solemn work to be done in lifting the standard high among those who have yet to hear the very first call to the gospel feast"—Letter 4, 1899.

In a manuscript titled "Work for This Time," Mrs. White wrote: "Christ preached the gospel to the poor, but He did not confine His labors to this class. He worked for all who would hear His word,— not only the publican and the outcasts, but the rich and cultivated Pharisee, the Jewish nobleman, the centurion, and the Roman ruler. This is the kind of work I have ever seen should be done. We are not to strain every spiritual sinew and nerve to work for the lowest classes, and make that work the all in all"—*Medical Ministry*, 312.

Speaking of Kellogg's work in Chicago, she said: "When you dipped into the work in the slums, to lift up the most degraded, you were not gathering with Christ as you supposed. I know that you may class me with your enemies because I tell you the truth. This truth may conflict with your ideas, but nevertheless, *it is the truth*" —Letter 232, 1899 (emphasis supplied).

She suggests how work for outcasts can be better done: "The Salvation Army workers are trying to save the neglected, downtrodden ones. Discourage them not. Let them do that class of work by their own methods and in their own way"—*Testimonies*, 8:185.

Mrs. White clearly states where the support for slum work should come from: "He [God] has not made it the special work of Dr. Kellogg to go into the worst dens of iniquity in the large cities. . . . If there are men who will take up the work of laboring for the most degraded, men upon whom God has laid the burden to labor for the masses in a variety of ways, let these converted ones go forth and gather *from the world* the means required to do this work. *Let them not depend on the means which God intends shall sustain the work of the gospel*"—Letter 205, 1899 (emphasis supplied).

This chapter in volume 6, has important principles regarding care for orphans: "Let those who have the love of God open their hearts and homes to take in these children." "If they have no relatives able to provide for them, the members of our churches should either adopt these little ones into their families or find suitable homes for them in other households" (281).

This is what Ellen White herself did. She took children into her home when necessary, and worked to find permanent homes for them. She considered that it was important for them to have a home setting to grow up in, rather than an institution. She said: "As far as lies in your power, make a home for the homeless" (284).

She did not urge ministers' wives to take responsibility for orphans, except under certain circumstances: "The question has been asked whether a minister's wife should adopt infant children. I answer: if she has no inclination or fitness to engage in missionary work outside her home, and feels it her duty to take orphan children and care for them, she may do a good work" (285).

Ellen White repeats her central point about orphan homes: "They are not to draw upon the people to whom the Lord has given the most important work ever given to men, the work of bringing the last message of mercy before all nations, kindreds, tongues, and people. The Lord's treasury must have a surplus to sustain the work of the gospel in 'regions beyond' " (286).

The period of many orphanages in the Seventh-day Adventist Church was relatively brief. There is still work to do for those less fortunate than ourselves. We are to feed the hungry, and clothe the naked, but we must not let such work divert us from our major goal of sharing the good news of salvation to all people.

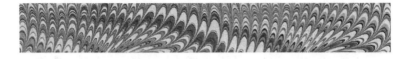

Introduction to Volume 7

1900-1902

In 1863, when the General Conference of Seventh-day Adventists was organized, there were 30 ministers, 3,500 members—all in North America—125 churches, no schools, no sanitariums or hospitals, no foreign missionaries, and one publishing house. By 1900, the church was working in thirty-nine languages, with thirteen publishing houses scattered around the world, 500 ministers, 1,000 other employees, 66,000 members, and nearly 1,900 churches.

The General Conference Committee had twelve members, only four of which lived in Battle Creek. Few decisions could be made—even in small matters—around the world, unless approved by these few men. In 1901, a General Conference session met at Battle Creek. Ellen White there called for a complete reorganization of the church, and Union Conferences were formed. The committee was enlarged to twenty-five members. And several departments were formed.

But the medical work was something else. Doctor Kellogg, its leader, was beginning to separate from the church. Then, on February 18, 1902, the main building of the Battle Creek Sanitarium burned to the ground.

Fires also destroyed the Review office late in 1902, and the Pacific Press in 1903. Both presses had accepted commercial printing, some of poor character, and other that contained doctrinal error. Ellen White had warned against such printing. The fires helped to get the message across. More will be considered from the next volume regarding these circumstances. From volume 7, a chapter has been chosen telling about a retirement plan for those who have served the church.

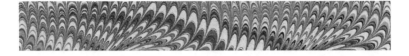

A Retirement Plan Is Born

7T 290-298

A two-part article by Ellen White appeared in *The Medical Missionary* magazine in June and July, 1891. The first article dealt with the need of an orphan's home, and the second one largely spoke of care for aged workers. In the second article, she recalled seeing—during her travels—provision made for war veterans: "As we travel, we see generous provision made for the veterans who fought in the war for our country. These men bear the scars of life-long infirmities that tell of their perilous conflicts, their forced marches, their exposure to storms, their suffering in prison. And all these give them a just claim upon the nation they helped to save,—a claim that is recognized and honored."

Then she asks: "But what provision have Seventh-day Adventists made for the soldiers of Christ? While we plead for a home for the orphans, we urge also that a minister's home should be provided."

She continues: "Our ministers who have labored earnestly, for-getful of self, to win souls to Christ, and who sink down in the battle wearied and ill, must not be left to struggle through life in poverty, or to feel that they are paupers."

More than the ministers are included: "The faithful laborers for God have for Christ's sake given up worldly prospects, choosing poverty rather than pleasure or riches; and when they are no longer able to labor, and have not means for their own support, it is but just that their wants *and the needs of those dependent upon them should be provided for*"—*The Medical Missionary*, July 1891(emphasis supplied).

Eleven years later (1902), a paper written by Ellen White was read at the Pacific Union Conference session, held at Portland, Oregon, February 28 to March 9. At that time the Union included Montana, Idaho, Washington, Oregon, California, Nevada, Utah, British Columbia, Hawaii, Arizona, and Alaska. There were nearly 10,000 church members in this large territory of about three and a half million inhabitants. In the paper, she expanded the list of those who should be cared for by the church: "Some provision should be made for the care of ministers *and others of God's faithful servants* who, through exposure and overwork in His cause, have become ill and need rest and restoration, or who, through age or loss of health, are no longer able to bear the burden and heat of the day" —*Pacific Union Recorder*, March 27, 1902 (emphasis supplied).

This presentation is the source of the chapter we are studying from the *Testimonies*.

The *Seventh-day Adventist Encyclopedia*, page 1027, states: "The first Seventh-day Adventist home for the aged was the James White Memorial Home in Battle Creek, Michigan. This home was operated from 1894 to 1905 on the same property as the Haskell Memorial Home" (the home for orphans).

This effort to care for the aged through a retirement home was a beginning. The first official record of action by the church regarding sustentation, or a retirement fund, came at the 1903 General Conference session. The proposal read as follows:

"Whereas, The tithe is the Lord's for the support of the gospel ministry,—

"Whereas, There is no well-defined general plan in operation for the support of aged or sick conference laborers, and the widows and orphans of deceased laborers; therefore,—

"We recommend, That all conferences and mission fields recognize the tithe as the inheritance of God's ministers, and that an allowance be granted from the tithe to properly support sick or aged laborers, also the widows and orphans of those removed by death"—*General Conference Bulletin*, 1903, 188.

A discussion by the delegates followed this recommendation, a discussion very strongly supporting it. The resolution was passed with only one slight amendment, inserting the word "dependent," reading as follows: "also the dependent widows and orphans of those removed by death."

It appears that no follow-up action was taken to implement the decision for seven more years, until the 1910 autumn council, December 4, 1910. At that time, a more detailed plan was developed—with Scripture support—as follows:

"Whereas, The Scriptures plainly teach—

1. That Israel, in the wilderness, under the leadership of Moses, was the recognized church of God (Acts 7:30);

2. That the Lord chose the Levites for the ministry of His church (Num. 3:6,7);

3. That the service of the sanctuary and the congregation was to be their sole occupation (verse 9);

4. That, because of their appointment to the Lord's work, they were His people, and He was their portion, in a special sense (Num. 3:45; 18:29);

5. That, because of their special relationship to God, and the service they were to perform, the Levites were not given an inheritance in the land, as were the other tribes (Deut. 10:8,9);

6. That instead of giving them a portion of the land for their inheritance, the tithe of all Israel was given to the Levites for their inheritance (Num. 18:21-24);

7. That this inheritance was given to them as a reward for the service they rendered to all the people (Num. 18:21, 31);

8. That all the people, including the Levites were to rejoice in this arrangement (Deut. 12:12);

9. That the people who had inheritance in the land were not to forget nor forsake the Levites who had none (Deut. 14:27);

10. That even to this day the tithe belongs to Christ, our great High Priest, for the support of those whom He calls to the gospel ministry (Heb. 7:4-9; 1 Cor. 9:7-14); and—

Whereas the adoption of this plan by Seventh-day Adventists provides a prompt, regular, and adequate support for the ministry, and,—

Whereas, in the application of this plan, no regular, well-defined arrangement has yet been made for the care of laborers who, because of serious illness, permanent illness, or old age, are unable to render full or even partial service, nor for the widows and children of those who fall in death at their post of duty; therefore,—

Resolved, That we hereby adopt, and recommend to all our conferences, the following plan,—

1. That we maintain a permanent fund, to be known as the Sustentation Fund, for the support of sick and aged laborers, and the widows and children of deceased laborers.

2. That the resource of this fund be the tithes of all our people.

3. That each local and union conference and the General Conference pay monthly into this Sustentation Fund an amount equal to five per cent of their total tithe receipts, these remittances to be made through the regular channels."

There was further provision made for a similar fund in other parts of the world. It was also suggested that aid be given in helping applicants to settle "where conditions will be most economical, where they can do the most to help maintain themselves, and where they may render the best service possible to the cause."

There was another interesting provision: "That any surplus funds on hand, above five thousand dollars, be appropriated annually to the General Conference for mission fields"—*Review*, December 22, 1910.

Local, union, and General Conference entities were to begin paying the 5 percent into the fund from January 1, 1911, and benefits would start February 1.

Today, there are many further refinements to the plan. Funds are disbursed on the basis of years of employment, and position, while active. Provision is made for assistance in relocation of retired workers, just as at the beginning. The choice of location, however, is that of the worker. And the range of church workers who are eligible for retirement benefits has grown. Anyone who has been regularly employed by the church can qualify for these benefits. In more recent years, the church health system operates its own retirement program.

It is perhaps easy for us to take for granted a retirement plan for those who have given years of service for a company or business. Those who have served their country in military service receive benefits too. Ellen White, remember, compared workers in God's cause to soldiers in the service of their country.

Ellen White suggests that church workers, in retirement should have "comfortable homes, with a few acres of land on which they can raise their own produce and feel that they are not dependent on the charities of their brethren"—*Testimonies*, 7:291, 292.

She counseled the church also to provide for the health needs of its retired workers. At that time, this may have been most readily provided by sanitariums or retirement homes. Today, the church provides for this, in principle, through a health insurance plan, supplementing social security.

The counsel is also to "be able to lay by a little from their salary, and this they should do, if possible, to meet an emergency" (293). She appeals to the aged to plan for the "right disposition" of their money before they die. Some can be given while they live, while other funds may be invested in God's cause after their death.

Ellen White has a great deal to say about retirement years. A compilation has been gathered from her writing, titled simply: *The Retirement Years*. Also, a chapter in *Selected Messages*, 2:221-232, provides valuable counsel.

Often, Mrs. White has suggested that there is value in the old and the young working together. Those who are young have en-

ergy and enthusiasm, that, combined with the wisdom and experience of the older, can accomplish much. We can all learn from
each other, and continue to share in giving the gospel as long as
life shall last. In 1890, she wrote: "The aged standard-bearers are
far from being useless and laid aside. They have a part to act in the
work similar to that of John. They can say, 'That which was from
the beginning, which we have heard, which we have seen with our
eyes, which we have looked upon, and our hands have handled, of
the Word of life; . . . that which we have seen and heard declare we
unto you, that ye also may have fellowship with us; and truly our
fellowship is with the Father, and with His Son Jesus Christ' "
—Manuscript 33, 1890 (*Selected Messages*, 2:223).

Introduction to Volume 8

1903, 1904

There have been several crises in the Seventh-day Adventist Church. But the pantheistic crisis in 1903 and 1904 was perhaps the most potentially devastating. This volume was published especially to meet that crisis.

The publishing house and the world headquarters moved from Battle Creek to Washington, D.C., in 1903. Repeatedly, Ellen White had served as a mediator between Kellogg and church administration. Sending counsels both to Kellogg and A. G. Daniells, president of the General Conference, she defended each man to the other, and at the same time continued messages of correction and reproof to both of them as well.

She had more than a passing interest in Kellogg's salvation. She and her husband, James, had helped to finance his medical training. She spoke of Kellogg as "the Lord's physician." And when it seemed that he was slowly drifting from the church, she gave both encouragement and frequent warnings to him.

But in an alarming way, Kellogg worked to separate the medical work from the church. He also began advancing pantheism, first in lectures, and finally, in a book titled *The Living Temple*.

Repeatedly, Mrs. White warned him against his pantheistic leanings. But he seemed to set himself more firmly in his beliefs, and in his determination to separate his work from the church. The whole situation was threatening to destroy the Seventh-day Adventist Church.

This eighth volume of *Testimonies* appeared in print during the Kellogg pantheism crisis. Much of its content was first written to him.

Warnings to Battle Creek

8T 48-122

The counsel in this section of *Testimonies for the Church*, volume 8, is all written to the Battle Creek church. For nearly fifty years, the headquarters of the Seventh-day Adventist Church was in Battle Creek. From 1855, when the church publishing was established there, until 1903, when both the administrative offices and the publishing house were moved to Washington, D.C., Battle Creek was the most significant Adventist center. During these years, thirty-four out of the first thirty-nine regular and special sessions of the General Conference were held there.

And Adventists congregated in ever-increasing numbers to work at the various institutions that were built. Building after building had been added. The Battle Creek Sanitarium especially was the hub around which so many church activities revolved. The medical work of the Sanitarium, under the direction of Doctor John Harvey Kellogg, drew many church members for employment. By the turn of the century, there were 2,000 members working for Kellogg, and only 1,500 for the rest of the church.

As noted in "The Times of Volume 8," this volume "was published to meet a crisis—the greatest crisis which the Seventh-day

Adventist Church has ever faced"—*Testimonies*, 8:5. It was published in March, 1904, only fifteen months after volume 7 was published. At the time of its appearance, some changes had already taken place. The publishing work and the church headquarters had been moved to Washington, D.C., and the college had moved to Berrien Springs, Michigan. But much more was needed.

Major fires had destroyed both the Battle Creek Sanitarium and the Review offices when this volume appeared. Kellogg, taken up with pantheistic teachings, was drawing the medical work away from the denomination. He was also resisting Ellen White's counsel, though she had been a lifelong friend and supporter of his work. Kellogg's growing defection posed a serious threat to the future of the church, not just its health ministry. More of this is considered in the next chapter.

For many years, Mrs. White had sent warnings against concentrating so many church institutions in Battle Creek. These warnings went largely unheeded. She finally decided to publish them in this form so that the entire church could read them. She speaks of "absorbing means, God's means, in one locality, when the Lord has spoken that too much was already invested in one place" (49).

At this point, she interjects other counsel. A fad was sweeping the country—bicycles. And Battle Creek Adventists had gotten caught up in it. She wrote: "I was shown things among our people that were not in accordance with their faith. There seemed to be a bicycle craze. Money was spent to gratify an enthusiasm in this direction that might better, far better, have been invested in building houses of worship where they are greatly needed. There were presented before me some very strange things in Battle Creek. A bewitching influence seemed to be passing as a wave over our people there, and I saw that this would be followed by other temptations. Satan works with intensity of purpose to induce our people to invest their time and money in gratifying supposed wants. This is a species of idolatry"—*Testimonies*, 8:51.

She continues: "There were some who were striving for the mastery, each trying to excel the other in the swift running of their bicycles. There was a spirit of strife and contention among them as to which should be the greatest" (52).

The bicycle fad has long since passed, but the use of time and money, and setting right priorities continue to be important. We might easily insert other fads that have come and gone into the place where it says "bicycle." Those possessions or activities that divert our attention from preparation for eternity, can be used by Satan to keep us from fulfilling our real purposes in this world.

But back to the major concern of this section. Not only were too many Adventists crowding into Battle Creek, but the work of the church needed to be built up in the rest of the world: "Altogether too much territory has been left unworked," Ellen White said. "The work is too much centralized. The interests in Battle Creek are overgrown, and this means that other portions of the field are robbed of facilities which they should have had" (59).

In another chapter, we reviewed the pioneering work that Ellen White's son, Edson, did among the Black population in the southern United States. Here she speaks of this "Southern field" as being neglected (60). Some money that was raised for Edson's work never got there. It was used in Battle Creek instead. She then compares Battle Creek with old Jerusalem: "Jerusalem is a representation of what the church will be if it refuses to walk in the light that God has given."

She speaks of Christ's messages to Jerusalem: "Her people perverted the truth, and despised all entreaties and warnings. They would not respect His counsels. The temple courts were polluted with merchandise and robbery. Selfishness and love of mammon, envy and strife, were cherished." Then application is made to Battle Creek: "He [Christ] comes to investigate in Battle Creek, which has been moving in the same track as Jerusalem. The publishing house has been turned into desecrated shrines, into a place of unholy merchandise and traffic. It has become a place where injustice and fraud have been carried on, where selfishness, malice, envy, and passion have borne sway."

How had the counsels been treated? "When warning and entreaties come to them, they say: 'Doth she not speak in parables?' Words of warning and reproof have been treated as idle tales" (67, 68). Mrs. White follows with an appeal to do medical missionary work. It is significant, however, that she urges that it should be spread throughout the world, and not centered in Battle Creek.

She returns to other dangers of too many Adventists in one place: "When Seventh-day Adventists move into cities where there is already a large church of believers, they are out of place, and their spirituality becomes weaker and weaker. Their children are exposed to many temptations."

She says further: "Many who have lived so long in one place are spending their time criticizing those who are working in Christ's lines to convict and convert sinners. They criticize the motives and intentions of others, as if it were not possible for anyone else to do the unselfish work they themselves refuse to do" (82).

A remedy is offered for such criticism: "If they would go to places where there are no believers, and work to win souls to Christ, they would soon be so busy proclaiming the truth and helping the suffering that they would have no time to dissect character, no time to surmise evil and then report the results of their supposed keenness in seeing beneath the surface" (82, 83).

Next, she speaks about commercial work that had been done at the Battle Creek publishing house. "Matter," she says, "of an objectionable character" should not be printed there. "Expensive machinery" should not be added only to do commercial work. Much of what was printed was not in harmony with our beliefs.

The next letter is addressed "To the Managers of the Review and Herald." Because of the corrupt material that was printed at the press, she spoke with a sense of foreboding: "I have been almost afraid to open the *Review*, fearing to see that God has cleansed the publishing house by fire" (91).

This fear was not long from becoming a reality. Writing to "The Brethren in Battle Creek" on January 5, 1903, she said: "Today I received a letter from Elder Daniells (General Conference president) regarding the destruction of the *Review* office by fire. I feel very sad as I consider the great loss to the cause. . . . But I was not surprised by the sad news, for in the visions of the night I have seen an angel standing with a sword as of fire stretched over Battle Creek."

She goes on: "Once, in the daytime, while my pen was in my hand, I lost consciousness, and it seemed as if this sword of flame were turning first in one direction and then in another. Disaster seemed to follow disaster because God was dishonored by the decision of men to exalt and glorify themselves" (97).

To understand the fulfillment of these visions, we turn to the newspaper accounts of the Haskell Home fire of February 5, 1909. The list of the many fires affecting Adventist institutions was a solemn reminder that Ellen White's vision of the angel with the "sword of flame . . . turning first in one direction and then in another," had met its fulfillment. Human causes for most of the fires were never discovered. Here is the list, from the *Battle Creek Journal*, February 5, 1909:

Date	Place	Loss
April 8, 1887	Washington Avenue 3 story Building	$5,000
June 1, 1891	Sanitarium Engine Room	$22,000
January 11, 1893	Battle Creek College Building	$7,000
February 3, 1896	Sanitarium Health Food Company	$13,000
July 19, 1898	Sanitarium Health Food Company	$10,500
April 12, 1900	Sanitary Nut Food Company	$5,200
July 21, 1900	Old Food Factory	$10,500
April 27, 1900	College Building	$5,300
February 18, 1902	Sanitarium and Hospital	$250,000
December 30, 1902	Review and Herald	$300,000
May 18, 1903	Sanitarium Barn	$4,000
July 10, 1905	Sanitarium Ice House	$1,800
February 5, 1909	The Haskell Home for Orphans	$60,000

There is still another fact that helps us to understand the setting of this counsel. Ellen White returned from a nine-year stay in Australia in 1900. The next year, 1901, a very significant General Conference session was held in Battle Creek. It was to be the last session ever held there. Major reorganization of the church was begun at that session. But not only was reorganization a necessity, there was need of reformation in the hearts and lives of those who were in leadership in the church. The next segment of this counsel to Battle Creek considers this need.

Mrs. White wrote of what "might have been done at the last General Conference if the men in positions of trust had followed the will and way of God." In a vision, she "seemed to be witnessing a scene in Battle Creek." She was in a meeting in the Tabernacle there, where it was clear that the Holy Spirit was present. Confessions of wrong were made by many attending. She says "It was a Pentecostal season" (104, 105). The meeting continued into the night until early morning.

When she returned to consciousness, she realized that it had only been a vision. The words were spoken: "This might have been." Then she knew that what she had witnessed "was not a reality" (105, 106). What a disappointment it was!

The final part of this section is titled "Forgetfulness." Here she compares the Battle Creek church to ancient Israel. She quotes several Bible passages, and then goes back to the 1844 experience: "If all who had labored unitedly in the work of 1844 had received the third angel's message and proclaimed it in the power of the Holy Spirit, the Lord would have wrought mightily with their efforts." Then a sobering conclusion is drawn: "Years ago the inhabitants of the earth would have been warned, the closing work would have been completed, and Christ would have come for the redemption of His people" (116).

What is to be learned from Israel? We turn to the Bible for the details. It is clear that they settled down without possessing the entire promised land. Joshua had been told by the Lord: "Every place that the sole of your foot shall tread upon, that have I given unto you, as I said to Moses" (Joshua 1:3).

But the whole land was not taken, and Israel paid a heavy price all of their years there, both in tribute and in the corruption of their beliefs through intermarriage and adoption of idol worship from the Canaanite nations. But they failed in another way later. They forgot their leaders, and the providences of God in their past history. The record says: "The people served the Lord all the days of Joshua, and all the days of the elders that outlived Joshua, who had seen all the great works of the Lord, that He did for Israel" (Judges 2:7).

When these early leaders were gone, they forgot the miraculous leading of God in establishing them there. Later, the Bible record says that "every man did what was right in his own eyes" (Judges 17:6).

Ellen White wrote long ago: "We have nothing to fear for the future, except as we shall forget the way the Lord has led us; and His teaching in our past history"—*Life Sketches*, 196.

We are on the borders of the heavenly promised land. We must learn from the past, or there will be further delay in entering the heavenly Canaan.

False Knowledge

8T 290-304

We have just considered Ellen White's counsel against too many Adventists settling in Battle Creek. Included is some specific concern for Doctor John Harvey Kellogg, superintendent of the Battle Creek Sanitarium, and his pantheistic teaching.

At the turn of the century, while Kellogg was beginning to separate his medical work from the Adventist Church, he was also advocating teachings that were not in harmony with established church beliefs. James and Ellen White had helped to finance his medical training, and had encouraged his health program from the start. He had been very supportive of them as well. From its beginning, in 1866, as the Western Health Reform Institute, to its accommodation of many hundreds at its peak, the Battle Creek Sanitarium had played a major role in the Adventist Church.

Kellogg became the director in 1876 at the early age of twenty-four. It was to be an association that would continue for sixty-seven years, until his death in 1943, at the age of ninety-one. And what a remarkable period of time it was! Doctor Kellogg also wrote more than fifty books. He established an orphanage, a retirement home, other sanitariums, a nursing school, and a medical college. He did inner-city work in Chicago for street derelicts. He edited several health journals, taught, traveled, and became a well-known surgeon. He developed several food products, including peanut butter, soy milk, a cereal coffee, and, of course, corn flakes. He patented several mechanical exercisers, electric light cabinets, and heat fomentations.

Few would challenge that Kellogg was a genius. The Battle Creek Sanitarium attracted many prominent people who came to learn more healthful habits, and to participate in his program. They included political figures William Jennings Bryan, and President of the United States, William Howard Taft ; entertainers Eddie Cantor, Percy Grainger, and Jose Iturbi; world-traveler Lowell Thomas; financial leaders, C. W. Barron, J. C. Penney, Montgomery Ward, S. S. Kresge, and Dale Carnegie; naturalist John Burroughs; philosopher-historian Will Durant; industrialists Alfred Dupont and John D. Rockefeller; grape juice producer Edgar Welch; horticulturist, Luther Burbank; the great inventor, Thomas Edison; educator, Booker T. Washington; songwriter Homer Rodeheaver; Admiral Richard Byrd; and aviatrix Amelia Earhart and many moore.

But problems began to develop between Kellogg and the church in several areas. Control of the medical program, and his doctrinal differences were the most prominent. Also he considered many of the ordained ministers as inferior to himself as a physician. He also claimed that they did not live up to healthful living principles. There was some basis in fact for this. And, in later years, though earlier he had been one of Ellen White's strongest allies, he turned against her counsel.

Kellogg's doctrinal differences included claiming that tithe could be given to any good cause that appealed to him. He also began to regard large portions of the Bible as figurative, particularly the prophecies. But the greatest concern was for his pantheistic beliefs regarding God. In his book, *The Living Temple*, he maintained that there is a divine presence in all living things. Many saw such a belief as destroying the distinctive Adventist doctrine of the heavenly sanctuary. Carried to its logical conclusion, this belief could lead to the conclusion that we are not responsible for our actions. Pantheism does away with a personal God.

Ellen White warned of the dangers in such a doctrinal position, and the majority of her counsel in this volume calls attention to these dangers. We might choose to study chapters from several sections. But we will concentrate on the chapter titled: "Dangers in Speculative Knowledge."

Interestingly, Mrs. White opened this volume in a positive way, urging that there were great evangelistic opportunities before the church, both in America and in other parts of the world— especially Europe (see Section 1, 9-47).

When Ellen White began to warn against too many interests of the church being centered in Battle Creek, some of those in charge of the work there, argued that it would not be practical to move away. Disastrous fires removed these objections for most. The college was moved to Berrien Springs in 1901, even before the fires. The Review office and church headquarters were moved to Washington, D.C., in 1903. But the sanitarium remained. In fact, Doctor Kellogg determined to rebuild on even a larger scale right in Battle Creek. To help raise money for the project, he authored the book, *The Living Temple*, with its subtle pantheistic teachings.

Satan has, from the beginning, sought to misrepresent God. In Eden he did this by challenging what God had said about the tree of knowledge. In pantheism, he teaches that God is in everything in nature—the sun, the trees, the grass. Carried to its logical end, God is in every human being, and therefore, we are above sin. Kellogg's book, *The Living Temple*, tended to elevate the human being to the level of God Himself. The appeal is obvious.

Pantheism had been presented regularly at Battle Creek College and the sanitarium. It appeared also at the 1903 General Conference session. But Ellen White did not address the issue there. In the autumn of 1903, however, visions instructed her to meet the pantheistic doctrine directly. She wrote from California to the autumn council in Washington, D.C., and her messages were read and accepted by nearly all who attended. But there was still perplexity among many church members. The publishing of volume 8 in March 1904, was a major factor in saving the church from further confusion and possible catastrophe.

When Ellen White published her counsels in the *Testimonies*, she did not usually identify those who were addressed. And the pantheistic crisis was no exception. She rarely names Doctor Kellogg, but readers were not left in doubt about who she was writing to, as she refers to "the medical superintendent of Battle Creek Sanitarium," "the managers of the Battle Creek Sanitarium," "to a physician in Battle Creek," "to the leaders in the medical work," etc. Sometimes she begins her letter "Dear Brother," or "to a physician in perplexity." All of these letters were written to Kellogg. In fact, the great majority of sections 3, 4, and 5 in this volume of the *Testimonies* were taken from letters, either to him or to those associated with him in the medical work in Battle Creek.

In section 5, "The Essential Knowledge," she deals specifically with the error of a wrong understanding of God. The chapter, "Danger in Speculative Knowledge," has been chosen from this section for our special attention.

Pantheism deals in speculation. There is nothing in Scripture to support such a concept of God. Ellen White states that Satan used "false science" or knowledge to deceive the angels in heaven. When he lost his place in heaven, he used the same temptation on our first parents. Ellen White says: "If Adam and Eve had never touched the forbidden tree, the Lord would have imparted to them knowledge, knowledge upon which rested no curse of sin, knowledge that would have brought them everlasting joy. All that they gained by their disobedience was an acquaintance with sin and its results" (290).

Satan, through the serpent, told half-truths at the tree of knowledge. He said: "Your eyes shall be opened, and ye shall be as gods, knowing good and evil." Adam and Eve's eyes were opened to sin and distrust of God and each other. But they did not become gods. They already knew "good." Now they became acquainted with "evil." Counterfeits are generally close to the genuine: "The path of error often appears to lie close to the path of truth" (290).

Our bodies are to be temples of the Holy Ghost, but this does not make us like gods. Mrs. White speaks of the end result of pantheistic belief: "The theory that God is an essence pervading all nature is one of Satan's most subtle devices. . . .They gratify the natural heart and give license to inclination" (291).

She goes on: "Our condition through sin has become preternatural, and the power that restores us must be supernatural, else it has no value" (291).

What does "preternatural" mean? The dictionary suggests that it means "abnormal." In order to be saved, the power must come from outside ourselves, not from within. Mrs. White says: "If God is an essence pervading all nature, then He dwells in all men; and in order to attain holiness, man has only to develop the power that is within him." What a dangerous deception! She says: "These theories, followed to their logical conclusion, sweep away the whole Christian economy. They do away with the necessity for the atonement and make man his own savior" (291).

The Bible says that we must be converted so that our bodies *can* become the dwelling place for God. We are not God. He made us in His image, but by sin we forfeited our perfect bodies.

Calling pantheism "fanciful views of God," Ellen White speaks of it as leading to "apostasy, spiritualism, and free-lovism" (292).

Mrs. White recalls fanaticism that developed soon after 1844. Some Adventists were active in teaching false ideas about God then. Among these was the idea that "those who were sanctified could not sin" (293). This "led to the belief that the affections of the sanctified would never lead astray." Immorality resulted. The same false concept is found in pantheism.

She goes on to warn that the past experience "will be repeated." The condition will be similar to the antediluvians. This is what is described: "The exaltation of nature as God, the unrestrained license of the human will, the counsel of the ungodly—these Satan uses as his agencies to bring about certain ends" (294).

The control of one mind by another is also a sure result. Note how Ellen White speaks of two things we "need" and two that we don't "need":

"At this time we *need* in the cause of God spiritually minded men."

"It is not new and fanciful doctrines which the people *need.*"

We "do not *need* human suppositions."

We "*need* the testimony of men who know and practice the truth" (294, 295).

The fruit of the forbidden tree in Eden was eaten for all the wrong reasons:

"The tree was good for food" (Satan's suggestion)

"It was pleasant to the eyes" (Eve allowed sense to rule her choice)

"Desired to make one wise" (Eve's desire ruled her knowledge).

These all had more to do with Eve's physical senses, than with her mind.

God's warnings were ignored. The serpent's lie was believed instead. No wonder that Ellen White says: "Pure and undefiled religion is not a sensational religion"—that is, dependent upon our physical senses (295). She says further: "God has not laid upon anyone the burden of encouraging an appetite for speculative doctrines and theories." She gets back to one of the greatest dangers in pantheism—that we will only follow our own inclinations, believing them to be safe: "Beware how you follow impulse, calling it the Holy Spirit" (296).

She continues: "Let none seek to tear away the foundations of our faith—the foundations that were laid at the beginning of our work by prayerful study of the word and by revelation." By "revelation" she means the visions that came to her.

She warns against two opposites: (1) "a hard, critical spirit," and (2) "false tests that Christ has never mentioned and that have no foundation in the Bible" (300).

Proverbs 3 has application here:

"Trust in the Lord with all thine heart; and lean not unto thine own understanding . . .

"Be not wise in thine own eyes . . .

"Honor the Lord with thy substance, and with the first fruit of all thine increase: so shall thy barns be filled with plenty, and thy presses shall burst out with new wine.

"My son, despise not the chastening of the Lord; neither be weary of His correction . . .

"Happy is the man that findeth wisdom, and the man that getteth understanding" (verses 5, 7, 9-11, 13).

These verses are often applied to stewardship of our possessions, but the context is our wisdom and our mind. It was difficult for someone with as great skills as Doctor Kellogg, to accept correction. Ellen White had such confidence in him that she once called him "the Lord's physician." But as Kellogg expanded his medical empire, he turned away from the counsel of the Lord.

In Eden, two trees were especially mentioned—the tree of knowledge, and the tree of life. The first was forbidden, the second was the true source of life. As sinners we tend to speculate about those things we do not understand. There is a tendency to form theories around such mysteries. When Darwin's *Origin of Species* appeared in 1859, it contained the theory of evolution. But though it generally contradicts the Bible, this theory has gradually been accepted by many as fact, instead of the Bible Creation account.

Satan tried to convince Eve that God was anti-intellectual. But such is not the case. Ellen White points out: "It was not His (God's) design that man should be content to remain in the lowlands of ignorance, but that he should secure all the advantages of an enlightened cultivated intellect"—*Testimonies*, 4:413.

It is sometimes claimed that Ellen White herself is opposed to intellectual pursuits. But this is not true either. She says: "Ignorance does not increase the humility or spirituality of any professed follower of Christ. The truths of the divine word can be best appreciated by an intellectual Christian"—*Counsels to Parents, Teachers, and Students*, 361.

And so, volume 8 proved to be a major factor in preserving the Seventh-day Adventist Church. Unfortunately, Doctor Kellogg chose to follow a different path. There were repeated attempts to reconcile with him. Ellen White was involved in some of these. But he was finally disfellowshipped on November 10, 1907.

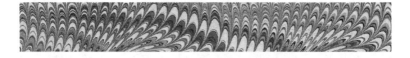

Introduction to Volume 9

1904-1909

This is the last of the volumes known as *Testimonies for the Church*. It was published during a period of recovery from the pantheistic crisis. The General Conference offices and the Review publishing office were now located in Washington, D.C. A sanitarium and college had been built there. Mrs. White lived in Washington for a few months in support of the move.

This was a period of major church development in several areas. A medical school was established at Loma Linda in 1905. Other medical facilities were also built in California. Large city work was developing, as was work among the Black population of the United States, in the south. Religious liberty work was also growing.

When this volume was published, Ellen White was eighty-one years of age. But she continued to participate in preaching and writing. Royalties from two books were committed by her for special needs. *The Ministry of Healing*, published in 1905, was to be used for the medical work of the church. *Christ's Object Lessons*, published in 1900, was to be used for debts on educational buildings.

Books that appeared from her pen after this volume, were *The Acts of the Apostles, Counsels to Teachers, Parents, and Students, Gospel Workers, Life Sketches*, and *Prophets and Kings*, published shortly after her death.

She fell and broke her hip on Sabbath, February 13, 1915, and was confined to bed for five months, finally resting from her work in death on July 16, 1915, at the age of eighty-seven. From this last volume, we look at her counsel about unity among nationalities and avoiding a spirit of independence.

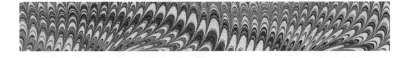

Unity Among
Different Nationalities

9T 179-183

The Seventh-day Adventist Church did not begin a worldwide mission program officially until 1874, when we sent J. N. Andrews to Europe. For many reasons, 1874 was a significant year. The modern advent movement had begun in 1844. In the thirty intervening years, many advances had been made. The 1840s was the decade when a system of doctrines was established, built on the Bible, with confirming visions through Ellen White. The 1850s had been the decade of organization. The 1860s saw the development of a comprehensive health message. And the 1870s saw the opening up of a worldwide work, with the actual presence of missionaries and institutions in countries other than the United States.

Probably Ellen White herself did not immediately realize the implications of two of her very early visions regarding a world witness. Fifty years later, she recalled her very first vision in December 1844, like this: "I saw a little glimmer of light and then another, and these lights increased and grew brighter, and multiplied and grew stronger and stronger till they were the light of the world"—MS 16, 1894 (quoted in *Selected Messages*, 3:64).

In a familiar vision at Dorchester, Massachusetts, in 1848, she was shown that we must begin a publishing work. She said: "From this small beginning it was shown to me to be like streams of light that went clear around the world"—*Life Sketches*, 125.

During the 1870s, Mrs. White began to have something more specific to say about a world work. She wrote in 1871: "Young men should be qualifying themselves by becoming familiar with other languages that God may use them as mediums to communicate His saving truth to those of other nations"—*Testimonies*, 3:204.

But "mission" areas were not only outside the United States. Writing in 1874, she said: "Our message is to go forth in power to all parts of the world—Oregon, England, Australia, to the islands of the sea, to all nations, tongues and peoples"—MS 1, 1874.

What was that again? Oregon a missionary territory? A quick check of history shows that the northern border of the northwest United States was not settled until 1846. In 1848, Oregon became a territory: in 1859 it became the thirty-third state. In 1877, three years after this statement by Ellen White, Chief Joseph, of the Nez Perce Indians, led a war against the white settlers in Oregon.

In a dream in 1874, Mrs. White saw the leaders of the church in council, considering how to plan for the future. An angel, appearing as a young man, spoke words that should still challenge us more than a century later: "Your light must not be put under a bushel or under a bed, but on a candlestick, that it may give light to all that are in the house. *Your house is the world*"—*Life Sketches*, 209 (emphasis supplied).

1874 was a significant year for still other reasons. We have already noted that J. N. Andrews went that year as our first foreign missionary. It was also the year we built our second publishing house, in California. And, perhaps even more important for a world work, we built our first college at Battle Creek that year. From the beginning, Ellen White saw the college as a place to train men and women for mission service.

The college was actually dedicated on January 4, 1875. We noted earlier that the day before, Mrs. White saw a developing work in many countries. Her attention was especially drawn to publishing houses. She spoke about this vision at the dedication ceremonies, and afterwards, recalled Australia as one of the countries in which she had seen publishing work. Ten years later, when she was in Europe she recognized publishing houses from this vision in Switzerland and Norway. When she went to Australia in 1891, she saw the publishing house there with her natural sight for the first time.

Writing to S. N. Haskell in 1875, she said: "Pamphlets and books should be prepared containing subject matter upon important points of present truth in English, German, French, Swedish, Danish, and Italian. Men of other nations and tongues should be educated as missionaries, translators and publishers . . . . The message of warning must be carried to every nation upon the globe" —Letter 34, 1875.

Remember, Ellen White herself went as a "missionary" to Oregon in 1878, and again in 1880 and 1884. In 1880, she also spent a short time in Canada. She went to Europe in 1885, working there for two years. And she spent the decade of the 1890s in Australia and New Zealand.

How did she counsel that such work should be done? We can observe five areas of counsel and practice from her own experience.

First, she was innovative. In Germany, for example, she writes of "breaking them in" to social meetings (testimony services). They had never been tried there, and proved to be successful (MS 32, 1887).

In Drammen, Norway, about thirty miles from Oslo, there was a church of twenty members. It had been difficult to get a hall for meetings while she was there. One was finally secured. Let's pick up her comments about it: "The best in the place was secured, a hall used for balls and concerts, about thirty-six by eighty feet in size, with a narrow gallery on each side and a huge stove in each end. There was no pulpit, nor a place for one. Six beer tables, brought in from an adjoining room, served to make a platform. A square carpet was thrown over this platform, and another table set on top for light stand and pulpit, while steps were made with chairs and stools."

Can you picture it? In a room that was often used for drinking, parties and concerts, we see Ellen White standing on six beer tables, preaching. Perhaps she smiled as she wrote: "We doubt if the hall or beer tables were ever put to so good use before"—*Historical Sketches of Foreign Missions of the Seventh-day Adventists*, 207.

At the European Union Council, a somewhat discouraging report was given from the Scandinavian colporteurs. The previous year barely $1,000 worth of books had been sold. Ellen White suggested that they conduct a four-month school in Stockholm, Sweden. Six hours in the middle of the day, they would sell books, and morning and evening training classes would be held. Twenty students enrolled, and the next year they sold more than $8,000 worth of books. A similar school was held in Basel, with Ellen White stating that she had been shown that some of the students would have positions of great responsibility in the future. This prediction was fulfilled. One later was president of the Latin Union Conference; another, president of the Swiss Conference, and others became preachers, translators, editors, teachers, and publishing house managers.

Second, she believed in starting right. The work was extremely hard in Europe at the beginning. Someone asked her: "Will there be some changes in conditions?" Her reply: "Yes, there will be some changes, but nothing for you to wait for."

She also warned against unwise economies. Though in Drammen, as just noted, they had gotten the best available hall for meetings, at other places she was disappointed with the meager arrangements. In Orebro, Sweden, she wrote: "The meeting hall consisted of a suite of chambers in the second story of a private dwelling. . . . The entrance was at the rear of the building. The principle room would accommodate about fifty persons; and two smaller ones, opening one into the other from this, would seat twenty each. All were furnished with board benches without backs.

It was clear that they didn't expect to attract a crowd. But she said: "The rooms were crowded to the utmost capacity." Ellen White continues: "I am convinced that we might have had a good hearing if our brethren had secured a suitable hall to accommodate the people; *but they did not expect much, and therefore did not receive much*" (emphasis supplied).

She concludes: "The character and importance of our work are judged by the efforts made to bring it before the public. When these efforts are so limited, the impression is given that the message we present is not worthy of notice"—ibid., 200.

Third, Ellen White recognized local conditions, needs and limitations. This principle is seen in her counsel regarding diet. She also recognized that the beginning work in some places would not be the same. In Europe, she encouraged publishing, and door to door book selling from the start, while in Australia she called for a strong health food development and a model college.

When she was in London, an incident illustrates her adaptability. She tells of being in a small hotel, planning for an early breakfast, which was her custom. A porter was paid to unlock the doors and bring dishes at 6:30 a.m. He was not used to so early an hour, and he did not wake up. Note her comment: "After this experience, we concluded that in order to enjoy traveling in Europe it was better to conform to the customs of the country than to try to introduce our own"—ibid., 167.

Fourth, she was practical. In Australia, she worked for orphans. It was a time of financial depression, and she bought furniture and other things at auctions to help neighbors. Dorcas meetings were held in her home to prepare food and clothing for those in need. At other times, she gave out dress material to mothers.

Fifthly, she opposed a nationalistic approach. And this brings us to our chapter. She recognized that in Europe it would not always be easy to preach our message. At the same time she rejoiced, even at the few who were faithful members. Her first Sabbath was spent at Grimsby, England. She recalls her Sabbath sermon: "Sabbath forenoon, when the little company of Sabbath-keepers assembled for worship, the room was full, and some were seated in the hall. I have ever felt great solemnity in addressing large audiences, and have tried to place myself wholly under the guidance of the Saviour. But I felt even more solemn, if possible, in standing before this small company, who, in the face of obstacles, of reproach and losses, *had stepped aside from the multitude* who were making void the law of God, and had turned their feet into the way of His commandments"—ibid., 162 (Emphasis supplied).

All of us "have stepped aside from the multitude" to become Adventists!

There was another incident in Sweden. It was 1885, and Mrs. White was traveling, along with her son W. C. White and Elder John Matteson. Matteson, whose home country was Sweden, was serving as her translator. It is apparent that her messages were troubling him, because he felt that her preaching was too strong on the Sabbath and the law. She was scheduled to preach on Sabbath, October 17. This is what she reported: "Brother E (Matteson) suggests that it would please the people if I speak less about duty and more in regard to the love of Jesus. But I wish to speak as the Spirit of the Lord shall impress me. The Lord knows best what this people needs. I spoke in the forenoon from Isaiah 58. I did not round the corners at all"—*Selected Messages*, 3:64.

Her diary account of this experience provides us with more details. A social meeting (testimony service) followed her sermon: "[They] expressed their thankfulness that the Lord sent them help from America and expressed their gratitude to God for the truth and for the increased light Sister White had given them. They could see, they said, as they had not done before, the necessity of greater strictness in keeping the Sabbath and could sense the offensive character of sin"—MS 26, 1885.

She recalls that "Brother Matteson interpreted." We might wonder at what went through his mind as her evaluation of the needs and interests of the congregation proved to be more appropriate than his.

How did Ellen White speak about work for various nationalities? Do these counsels have to do with our work for racial and ethnic groups as well? The chapter we are studying comes from her address at the European Union Council at Basel, Switzerland, the first she attended after arriving in Europe.

She says that some who had gone to Europe before her believed that people of different countries have to be dealt with in certain ways. But she did not agree totally. Her comments are worth noting: "Though some are decidedly French, others decidedly German, and others decidedly American, they will be just as decidedly Christlike"—*Testimonies*, 9:180.

Then she draws a lesson from the building of the Jewish temple, reminding us that the stones were fitted before they were brought to the temple site, where there was no sound of ax or hammer: "This building represents God's spiritual temple, which is composed of material gathered out of every nation, and tongue, and people, of all grades, high and low, rich and poor, learned and unlearned" (180).

She goes on to make a point: "Therefore God wants the different nationalities to mingle together, to be one in judgment, one in purpose. Then the union that there is in Christ will be exemplified" (180,181).

She speaks of being almost afraid to come to Europe because she had heard that the many nationalities were "peculiar and had to be reached in a certain way." But, she reminded them, "there are not six patterns," but one, "and that is Christ Jesus." She said: "If the Italian brethren, the French brethren, and the German brethren try to be like Him, they will plant their feet on the same foundation of truth." She asks them not to build up "a wall of partition between different nationalities" (181).

While in Australia, she had emphasized the same point, saying "there are two distinct classes" of people: "Those who are saved through faith in Christ and through obedience to His law, and those who refuse the truth as it is in Jesus." She urged: "Caste and rank are not recognized by God, and should not be by His workers. The test will come not as regards the outward complexion, but as regards the condition of the heart"—*Review*, April 2, 1895.

Writing about the work in the United States she emphasized the same truth: "In Christ Jesus we are one. By the utterances of one name 'Our Father,' we are lifted to the same rank . . . . In our worship of God there will be no distinction between rich and poor, white and black. All prejudice will be melted away. When we approach God, it will be as one brotherhood"—ibid., October 24, 1899.

We could say that Ellen White's great concern was for unity in the faith. That's what this address in Europe was all about. But the application is not limited to Europe. It is for all of us as God's children, wherever we are.

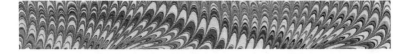

The Spirit of Independence

9T 257-261

Ellen White read the contents of this chapter to the delegates at the 1909 General Conference session in Washington, D.C. She recalled her return to America from Australia, in 1900, observing that "only a few of the pioneers of the cause now remain among us." She speaks of the burdens of the work "falling upon younger men" and expresses a major concern: "The spirit of pulling away from fellow laborers, the spirit of disorganization is in the very air we breathe. By some, all efforts to establish order are regarded as dangerous—as a restriction of personal liberty, and hence to be feared as popery. These deceived souls regard it a virtue to boast of their freedom to think and act independently."

The presentation continues: "I have been instructed that it is Satan's special effort to lead men to feel that God is pleased to have them choose their own course independent of the counsel of their brethren." Then, a look to the future: "Some have advanced the thought that, as we near the close of time, every child of God will act independently of any religious organization. But I have been instructed by the Lord that in this work there is no such thing as every man's being independent" (257).

"It is not a good sign," she says, "when men refuse to unite with their brethren and prefer to act alone" (258). But Ellen White often encouraged independent thinking, and she does so in this presentation: "On the other hand," she says, ". . . brethren in responsibility should be slow to criticize movements that are not in perfect harmony with their methods of labor" (259).

She uses Ezekiel's vision of wheels within wheels to illustrate how God works through a variety of persons, who can yet be in harmony if directed by Him. Speaking about the General Conference, she says: "I have often been instructed by the Lord that no man's judgment should be surrendered to the judgment of any other one man" (260).

The past is recalled, when a small group of men controlled most major decisions: "I have said that I could no longer regard the voice of the General Conference, *represented by these few men*, as the voice of God" (Emphasis supplied).

This is followed by a balancing statement: "But this is not saying that the decisions of a General Conference composed of an assembly of duly appointed, representative men from all parts of the world field should not be respected. God has ordained that the representatives of His church from all parts of the earth, when assembled in a General Conference, shall have authority" (261).

She then concludes: "Let us give to the highest organized authority in the church that which we are prone to give to one man or to a small group of men."

What conditions called for such cautions? In the decade of the 1890s, the Seventh-day Adventist Church more than doubled in membership from 29,000 to over 66,000. But it was also a time of crisis. With world work rapidly developing, many educational, health, and publishing institutions were established. Following the 1888 General Conference session, where righteousness by faith had been so powerfully presented, doctrinal controversy flared, with strong opinions on both sides. Most of the church leaders eventually accepted the righteousness by faith emphasis, but there were notable exceptions.

In publishing, efforts were being made by some church administrators to control all world publishing houses from Battle Creek. Here we find the names of A. R. Henry and Harmon Lindsay. Who were these men, and what did Ellen White say about them?

Harmon Lindsay was the General Conference treasurer in 1874-1875 and again from 1888-1893. He was also a financial advisor for Battle Creek College, Oakwood College, and the Central Publishing Association. He later left the church and joined the Christian Scientists.

A. R. Henry was General Conference treasurer from 1883-1888. In addition, he served, between 1882 and 1897 at times as president, vice-president, treasurer and auditor of the General Conference Association. He was also manager and treasurer of the Central Publishing Association. He actually served on eleven boards, including Battle Creek College, the Sanitarium, and the foreign mission board. At the same time, he had extensive personal business interests.

When he was not reelected to the Publishing Association board in 1897, Henry brought two $50,000 lawsuits against the board. The first alleged that testimonies written by Ellen White, and circulated among church leaders by O. A. Olsen (*Special Testimonies*, Series A), were so libelous that the board had dismissed him. The second suit, also against the Publishing Association, claimed that he had been underpaid as vice-president, treasurer, and manager for fifteen years. These suits proved an embarrassment to the church.

Neither of these men accepted the emphasis on righteousness by faith at Minneapolis. Speaking about Henry, Ellen White said: "Since the Minneapolis meeting he has never taken his position in full reception of the light God has so graciously given for these last days. He has not honored the position he has occupied in the Office, because he has carried the spirit of A. R. Henry in full size"—Letter 2, 1894 (quoted in *Manuscript Releases*, 17:171,172).

In the same letter, she speaks of the problems created when O.

A. Olsen, president of the General Conference, chose these men as close advisors: "The Lord has a controversy with them, and yet Elder Olsen treats them as representative men, sending them hither and thither as men of discernment, endorsing them as trustworthy and reliable men, to whom the people shall listen and show respect as the voice of God in the Conference"—ibid.

Speaking more directly about the publishing house at Battle Creek, and these men, she said: "I could not entrust the light God has given me to the publishing house at Battle Creek. I would not dare to do this. As for your book committee, under the present administration, with the men who now preside, I would not entrust to them for publication in books the light given me of God, until that publishing house has men of consecrated ability and wisdom. As for the voice of the General Conference, there is no voice from God through that body that is reliable"—MS 57, 1895.

She repeatedly identified Henry and Lindsay in her correspondence: "When men like A. R. Henry and Harmon Lindsay refuse to be worked by the Holy Spirit, and yet consent to accept important responsibilities, Satan takes possession of their minds, and plans and devises for them"—Letter 4, 1896.

Speaking of their taking rightful royalties from authors, Ellen White wrote: "This seemed to be a subject upon which A. R. Henry was crazed, but his enthusiasm was the inspiration of Satan, and by the influence of the tempter the moral depravity has spread till there is danger that it will corrupt every right principle in the life of Brother Henry. Harmon Lindsay is no more pure in his integrity than is A. R. Henry."

In the same letter she says: "I saw that they had visited Brother (Uriah) Smith and obtained his consent to a low royalty in order that they might present this as that which I and others should do. This was obtaining terms of royalty by fraud."

Under the leadership of these men, the publishing house gave preference to commercial work that was often corrupt. She spoke of this too: "Books that should have been circulated in these critical times have been put aside until the worldly work had first been finished"—MS 124, 1901.

Ellen White clearly states why she lacked confidence in the General Conference during the decade of the 1890s: "This is the reason I was obliged to take the position that there was not the voice of God in the General Conference management and decisions. Methods and plans would be devised that God did not sanction, and yet Elder Olsen made it appear that the decisions of the General Conference were as the voice of God. Many of the positions taken, going forth as the voice of the General Conference have been the voice of one, two, or three men who were misleading the conference"—MS 33, 1891.

During this decade Ellen White wrote many letters from Australia to O. A. Olsen and other leaders, regarding the problems at the General Conference. Elder Olsen printed many of these communications in a series of pamphlets, before mentioned. *Testimonies to Ministers* is largely taken from these letters.

But this is not the first time that too much authority was assumed by individuals in the General Conference. In the 1870s, when G. I Butler was president of the General Conference, he regarded the presidency as giving him rather absolute power. Writing to him, Ellen White had given similar counsel: "I have been shown that no man's judgment should be surrendered to the judgment of any other man. But when the judgment of the General Conference, which is the highest authority that God has upon the earth, is exercised, private independence and private judgment must not be maintained, but be surrendered."

She goes on: "You considered it a virtue in you to persistently maintain your position of independence. You did not seem to have a true sense of the power that God has given to His church in the voice of the General Conference"—*Testimonies*, 3:492.

Ellen White, herself, recognized that "voice" when she traveled to Australia in 1891 at the request of the General Conference: "I had not one ray of light that He [God] would have me come to this country. I came in submission to the voice of the General Conference, which I have ever maintained to be authority"—Letter 124, 1896.

But something changed soon after. Several times during the 1890s, she questioned that authority. Note a sample of comments from her pen:

"As for the voice of the General Conference, there is no voice from God through that body that is reliable"—MS 57, 1895.

"The sacred character of the cause of God is no longer realized at the center of the work. The voice from Battle Creek, which has been regarded as authority in counseling how the work should be done, is no longer the voice of God"—Letter 4, 1896.

"The councils at this great center [Battle Creek], if kept pure and uncorrupted, would have been as the voice of God; but men have worked upon principles that are condemned by the word of God, and they have not heard nor obeyed the voice of God" —Letter 71, 1898.

"As I was made to understand something of the management of the work in this great center, it was all that I could bear. My spirit was pained within me, for I had lost confidence in that which I had ever presented before the people as the voice of God to His children. It has not been the voice of God. . . . We cannot therefore present before the people that the voice of the General Conference in its decisions must move and control them; for its propositions and decisions cannot be accepted"—MS 66, 1898.

To further complicate the situation, A. W. Stanton published a tract "The Loud Cry! Babylon is Fallen!" in 1893. This tract characterized the Seventh-day Adventist Church as Babylon, calling God's "true people" to come out of her. Ellen White's response was immediate: "Beware of those who arise with a great burden to denounce the church. The chosen ones who are standing and breasting the storm of opposition from the world, and are uplifting the downtrodden commandments of God to exalt them as honorable and holy, are indeed the light of the world. How dare mortal man pass his judgment upon them, and call the church a harlot, Babylon, a den of thieves? . . .

"When anyone is drawing apart from the organized body of God's commandment-keeping people, when he begins to weigh the church in his human scales, and begins to pronounce judgment against them, then you may know that God is not leading him. He is on the wrong track"—MS 21, 1893.

And so, though correction was needed by the church and some of its leaders, it was not a time to begin a new church, but to correct evils in it. More can be read about Stanton's challenge in the first section of *Testimonies to Ministers*, pp. 15-62.

Correction and reproof through the prophetic voice to the church is frequently used by critics to discredit the church. But that voice does not point out wrongs, and then say: "I'm telling you this just before God destroys you." The exact opposite is true. God says, to the last church of Laodicea: "As many as I love, I rebuke and chasten; be zealous therefore, and repent" (Revelation 3:19). The modern messenger does the same. Note her statement in 1867: "God loves His people who keep His commandments, and reproves them, not because they are the worst, but because they are the best people in the world"—*Testimonies*, 1:569.

As the church gathered for the General Conference session of 1901, Mrs. White issued an urgent appeal for reorganization of the church, with these words:

"That these men should stand in a sacred place, to be the voice of God to the people, as we once believed the General Conference to be—that is past. What we want now is a reorganization. We want to begin at the foundation, and to build upon a different principle"—*General Conference Bulletin*, April 3, 1901.

The men who had so dominated church policy for more than a decade, would no longer have leadership positions. Their influence largely disappeared. Not everything was accomplished that was needed in reorganization, but there was a strong beginning. From that time on, Ellen White spoke of a positive future for the church. In 1905 she wrote: "We cannot now step off the foundation that God has established. We cannot now enter into any new organization; for this would mean apostasy from the truth"—*Selected Messages*, 2:390.

In 1908 she said: "I am instructed to say to Seventh-day

Adventists the world over, God has called us as a people to be a peculiar treasure unto Himself. He has appointed that His church on earth shall stand perfectly united in the Spirit and counsel of the Lord of hosts to the end of time"—ibid., 397.

Then, in 1909, she published this chapter we are studying, confirming that "God has ordained that the representatives of His church from all parts of the earth, when assembled in a General Conference, shall have authority" (261).

What can we conclude? We are to work together in unity, and yet we are not to allow ourselves to be dominated by anyone else. A wrong "spirit of independence" can be demonstrated by church leaders as well as individual members. We are still to honor the voice of the General Conference as authority when representatives "from all parts of the earth" are assembled. Ellen White's presentation concludes on this note: "Let us give to the highest organized authority in the church that which we are prone to give to one man or to a small group of men" (261).

We can better understand the implications of this statement looking back to the time when the work of the church was controlled by only a few men, who were not under the direction of the Holy Spirit. Ellen White showed her confidence in the Seventh-day Adventist Church in her last will, entrusting her writings to the church, and a Board of trustees that included the president of the General Conference, A. G. Daniells. Her writings continue to be cared for by the church through the Ellen G. White Estate Board.

In 1913, two years before her death, Ellen White wrote: "I am encouraged and blessed as I realize that the God of Israel is still guiding His people, and that He will continue to be with them, even to the end"—*Life Sketches*, 437, 438.

Epilogue

For seventy years, the Seventh-day Adventist Church was favored by God with a living prophetic messenger. Through letters, sermons, articles, personal interviews, and books, Ellen White faithfully gave "testimonies" she had received through visions from the Lord. Her personal ministry to both the church and to individuals is a matter of record. She did not always find it easy to give these testimonies--whether to church leaders, to her family, or to the general membership. There were many individuals who did not find it easy to accept them either. But with the passing of time, the testimonies have clearly been found to be of divine origin.

Those who chose to reject these testimonies, for whatever reasons, have always been the losers. They have usually left the church. Those who have accepted them have been blessed and prospered spiritually. This is also demonstrated in the testimonies given by Bible prophets.

It was usually easy in Bible times to look back and confirm that the prophet's messages were right. The religious leaders in Christ's day claimed to believe "the prophets." But they found it more difficult to accept Christ, the greatest of the "prophets." Human nature is still the same in our day.

The messages of the prophets are part of a continuing effort by God to help us on our way to the heavenly kingdom. These "testimonies" are not only better understood when we know why they were given but can be applied personally in each of our lives. They are consequently of more than historical interest. They are "for our admonition, upon whom the ends of the world are come."